MOTHER
FATHER

MOTHER
FATHER

Harry A. Wilmer, Editor

With the assistance of Elizabeth Silverthorne

Robert Bly • Elisabeth Kübler-Ross • Mary Catherine Bateson • Betty Sue Flowers • Jerome Kagan • Elizabeth Silverthorne • Mary Briner • John Silber • Murray Stein • Harry Wilmer • Harry Wilmer III

Chiron Publications • Wilmette, Illinois

Library of Congress Catalog Card Number: 89–36876

Printed in the United States of America.
Copyedited by Maryann Kannapran and Siobhan Drummond Granner.
Book design by Michael Barron.

Grateful acknowledgment is made for the following permissions:

Elisabeth Kübler-Ross, "On Being Born, On Caring, and On Dying." © copyright 1989 by Elisabeth Kübler-Ross. Published with the author's permission.
John Silber, "The Myth of the Hero." © copyright 1989 by John Silber. Published with the author's permission.
Murray Stein, "The Significance of Jung's Father in His Destiny as a Therapist of Christianity," *Quadrant*, vol. 18, no. 1 (Spring 1985). Reprinted with permission by the C. G. Jung Foundation for Analytical Psychology.
Harry A. Wilmer, "Jung: Father and Son," *Quadrant*, vol. 18, no. 1 (Spring 1985). Reprinted with permission by the C. G. Jung Foundation for Analytical Psychology.
Portions of Mary Catherine Bateson, *With a Daughter's Eye: A Memoir of Margaret Mead and Gregory Bateson* (New York: Wm. Morrow and Co., 1984) are reprinted with permission by the author.
Portions of Jerome Kagan, *The Nature of the Child* (New York: Basic Books, 1984) are reprinted with permission by the author.

Library of Congress Cataloging-in-Publication Data:
Mother, father / Harry A. Wilmer, editor; with the assistance of
  Elizabeth Silverthorne . . . [et al.].
    p.   cm.
  ISBN 0-933029-45-4
  1. Parent and child. 2. Mothers. 3. Fathers. I. Wilmer, Harry A., 1917–   .
II. Silverthorne, Elizabeth, 1930–   .
HQ755.85.M68 1989   89-36876
                                                                        CIP

ISBN 0–933029–45–4

Dedication

Leona S. Wilmer
Harry A. Wilmer I

Contents

Preface

It somehow seems appropriate that my father would ask me to write the preface to a book edited by him titled *Mother Father*. I will avoid the attempt to provide revealing insight or interpretation of the following chapters that deal with the masculine and the feminine spirit. I believe that they speak well for themselves.

I would, however, like to reflect for a moment upon some of my experiences and observations as the oldest son of my father who is the founder and spirit behind the Institute for the Humanities at Salado. The Institute itself has experienced a remarkable and consistent sense of balance and avoided the pitfalls and excesses usually associated with success. It is dedicated to quality and exploring the humanities with experts sharing their ideas and observations with people in a nonacademic setting in a small rural community in central Texas.

When I suggested in 1969 that my parents buy a house in Salado, it was a very fortuitous event, including, I believe, the first time my father followed the advice of his son rather than the reverse. Salado is such an unlikely place to have symposiums on Vietnam, the Myths of Texas, and Understanding Evil, plus a lecture series each spring and each fall on various topics including the series, "My Mother/My Father, The Feminine and Masculine Spirit," which is the basis for this book. It is perhaps just because Salado is such an unlikely place that it provides a unique and fresh perspective on the world of ideas and the humanities and their meaning.

I have been very fortunate to have grown up with exposure to this remarkable world of ideas and the humanities. Coincidentally, one of my early memories as a young boy was visiting Gregory Bateson, the father of Mary Catherine Bateson. I spent hours being interviewed by Gregory Bateson who had an office at the local V. A. hospital in Menlo Park, California, near where we lived. As I recall, he asked questions, discussed and diagrammed things I really didn't understand about family roles and relationships with my brothers, my mother and my father. I suppose he was trying to understand behavior patterns and customs that the rest of the world simply took for granted. He questioned things that a young boy of seven or eight would surely never question on his own. He awakened a sense of self-awareness as I first explored the inner world of ideas and feelings, the conscious and the unconscious that was my father's world.

There is an interesting parallel between Carl Jung's father and mine. Jung's father has been described as both a representative and a victim of an ailing religious tradition. I believe that my father was both a representative and a victim of an ailing Freudian tradition. It was painful to see my father trapped and struggling as the captive of Freudian psychoanalysis. His analyst advised him against making any significant decisions or changes until his analysis was complete—a real paralysis of analysis. My father was trapped in this introspective black hole until he discovered the world of Carl Jung. It still took a lot of courage to finally reject the Freudian dogma that was widely embraced at the time. His rejection of the Freudian world and belief system was also the entrance into a more well-balanced world that began a very creative and productive stage of my father's life.

It was probably because of my father's experience that I had the good fortune to experience an escape from being caught up in a similar introspective psychological black hole. By the age of twenty-one, I finally concluded that no matter what my mother and my father may or may not have done, I was ultimately responsible for my own behavior, success, and failure. It simply was up to me to make the most of whatever psychological and genetic gifts and limitations were passed on to me by my mother and my father.

Perhaps my father was inherently irreverent and a risk taker. He has taken tremendous risks throughout his career, facing and dealing with the dark side, that few even acknowledge. These risks included an experiment with the therapeutic community for treating psychotic Korean War Veterans at the Oak Knoll Naval Hospital in Oakland, California; therapeutic community to prepare prisoners for parole from San Quentin Prison in California; a treatment program for the hippies from Haight Asbury on a drug ward at Langley Porter with the University of California Medical School in San Francisco; studying dreams of Vietnam Veterans at a V. A. hospital in San Antonio; and a therapy program to help AIDS patients deal with death and dying at the University of Texas Health Science Center in San Antonio. I think what I learned most from my father is that most problems are hidden opportunities and more people would recognize opportunity if it didn't come disguised as a challenge and hard work.

Our relationship was not without a great deal of strain. As a young man, it was always easier to communicate if I needed assistance on some emotional or academic problem. My father's world was the one of the psychological and the academic. Therefore, a problem in one of these areas was a ticket for a more meaningful visit.

On the academic side, the most meaningful thing I learned was that the divisions between the academic disciplines were artificial. There are no real barriers between psychology, sociology, anthropology, literature, art, history, economics, etc. The disciplines are systems created to help categorize, organize, study and understand human behavior. The separation between these fields of study are mythical creations in the minds of man and they are only true because of a system of common belief. These disciplines are simply ways of developing different ways of thinking and understanding the world around us whether in the sciences or the humanities. To truly understand the real world it helps to recognize that these disciplines are part of a continuum and to understand that the interconnections and interrelationships provide more meaningful perspective and comprehension. We are, after all, a function of our knowledge and beliefs and our consciousness and unconsciousness. However we think and process our culture, it is our values, language, and what we believe that makes us what we are.

Harry A. Wilmer III

Acknowledgment

The contributions by Mary Catherine Bateson, Robert Bly, Jerome Kagan, and Elisabeth Kubler-Ross are adapted from lectures that they delivered at the fall 1985 lecture series of the Institute for the Humanities at Salado. John Silber's chapter is based on his lecture at the 1984 symposium, "Texas Myths: The Personal and the Collective Mythology," at the Salado Institute. Betty Sue Flowers and Elizabeth Silverthorne, both members of the Board of Trustees of the Salado Institute, wrote their chapters at the request of the editor. Mary Briner, in Zürich, prepared her contribution from a series of lectures and seminars that she delivers at the C. G. Jung Institute in Zürich and Küsnacht. This was a special concession to the editor as she has never published any of her seminars or lectures before.

The Institute for the Humanities at Salado is grateful to Chiron Publications for their publication of the series of books on lectures from the Salado Institute. The next volumes will be: *Creativity Alive and Well*, and *The Human Spirit, The Healing Spirit*. The help of Murray Stein, Nathan Schwartz-Salant, and Chiron editors Siobhan Drummond Granner and Maryann Kannapran is acknowledged.

The Salado Institute thanks the following foundations for grants which made the programs, lectures, and book possible: The Rockwell Fund, Inc., Houston; The Texas Committee for the Humanities, Austin (a state program of the National Endowment for the Humanities); The Kemnner Fund, Galveston; The Brown Foundation, Inc., Houston; The Harris Foundation, Chicago; and the Hogg Foundation, Austin.

Introduction

The essays in this book with two exceptions were adapted from lectures and discussions at the Institute for the Humanities at Salado, Texas. The book is divided into two sections: *Part I: My Mother, My Father*, and *Part II: The Mother, The Father*. This is no subtle distinction. Personal mothers and personal fathers are seen through the eyes of their children, now grown and famous in their own right. While the children were growing up, the parents were also growing and as Mary Catherine Bateson once said, "It is almost the same thing as with children. We never know how our parents are going to turn out as they grow in age." The essays in this book are about famous parents or by famous children now parents themselves. A reporter for the *New York Times* once interviewed Leonard Bernstein's father. As I remember the article, he asked the old man why he had discouraged his son from following a musical career. The father replied, "How did I know he was going to turn out to be Leonard Bernstein?" What a wonderful line—not turn out to be a great musician or conductor but to be himself! In the western world we are saddled with some general principles and doctrines about love, affection, and relationship of child and parent. Some of these cherished beliefs are challenged by Jerome Kagan in his hopeful, brilliant, and somewhat distressing chapter.

"My Mother, My Father" refers to real people, in real time and space, but "The Mother, The Father" relates to transpersonal mothers and fathers, to parental imagos, surrogates, historical mothers and fathers, archetypal mothers and fathers, the mythology of mother and infant, child and father. "Our Father Who Art in Heaven" is not our father who is on earth, alive or dead. The eternal mother, the eternal feminine, the eternal father, the eternal masculine are part of everyone's psyche. In Jungian psychology these may be known as the anima and the animus, the soul. But one thing is certain—the essential power of our real parents is derived from forces beyond their human mortal beings. But let us return to our real parents.

My own father was Harry A. Wilmer, I was called Harry A. Wilmer II. I called my son Harry A. Wilmer III, but rarely referred to him in that manner except in publications where our identical names appear. These Roman numerals not only separate but indicate a continuity of fathers and sons. My own father delighted in being identified as "Big Harry" and called me "Little Harry," "Harry Junior," or "Harry the Second." And I thought I was both belittled and unduly associated with royalty. It was both an inflation and a deflation. Now I know being big is sometimes being small.

I was surprised when my son, Harry A. Wilmer III, who wrote the preface to this book, talked of a similarity between him and me and Jung and his father. We have much to learn from our children.

My father always showed warmth and demonstrable affection. He would embrace me, kiss me, hug me. Warmth, demonstrable affection, and touching are considered essential needs of infants and children for their health and development in the early moments of life, but after that? Do we need to show unconditional love by the active display of affection to our children or those we care for as children (the sick and the suffering)? Elisabeth Kubler-Ross personifies the loving touching relating physician, woman and human spirit, but is it necessary that we should also be that way? Is unconditional love identified by personal affectionate relationships? Jerome Kagan makes us wonder.

As a man I cannot really know what it is to gestate, deliver, and nurse a child, but I have loved my children and my wife and given birth to things, ideas, books, and dedicated them to mothers, fathers, and children. *Huber the Tuber: The Lives and Loves of a Tubercle Bacillus* (1942) was dedicated to "The memory of my father who always was and always shall be my greatest inspiration." I dedicated *This Is Your World* (1952) as follows: "This one is for John, three, because he wants it most. I wish it were for Hank, five, because he was the first. And there is Tom, two—lucky number three." *Social Psychiatry in Action* (1958) was dedicated this way: "For my wife and our children: Harry, John, Thomas, James, Mary." And this book is dedicated to both my father and my mother. The cycle is full.

My book *This Is Your World* contains a ballad I wrote and illustrated. One picture was titled "Remember when?" It is a montage of memory images of my son Hank then, from birth to five, showing the birth of his brother, John, and Jane is taking pictures with a box camera. Hank holds a piece of bread and you can see his left eye looking at himself at the age of one week. Below this I am carrying him (Figure 1).

When Ilya Tolstoy was 70 years of age, he wrote an important and loving biography entitled *Tolstoy, My Father: Remembrances* (Chicago: Cowles Book Co., Inc., 1971). It was this book that stimulated me to bring these speakers to Salado, Texas, to talk to the Salado Institute. Three paragraphs in Ilya Tolstoy's book made an especially deep impression on me.

> *Papa* was the cleverest man in the whole world. He too knew everything, but it was impossible to be naughty with him. Later, when I had learned how to read, I found out that he was a "writer." I happened to like some lines of poetry I had read, and asked *maman* who had written them. She told me that they were by Pushkin, and that he was a great writer. I felt disconsolate that my father wasn't a writer. And when she told me that he was a famous writer too, it made me very happy. (p. 15)

Figure 1. From *This is Your World*, p. 68.

Remember when?

> I never witnessed a single expression of tenderness on the part of my father during his lifetime. Kissing children was something he did not like and did only as a duty when greeting us. It was therefore understandable that he did not attract tenderness from others, and that the feeling of closeness to him was never accompanied by any outer manifestation. It would never have occurred to me, for instance to go up to my father and kiss him or stroke his hand. This was partly because of my awe of him and partly because of his spiritual power and greatness, which prevented me from seeing him simply as a man who at times was pitiful and weary, a weak old man so much in need of warmth and rest.
>
> The only person who could give him that warmth was Masha [his daughter]. She would go to him and stroke his hand, caress him, say an affectionate word, and one could see that it pleased him, and made him happy, and he even returned her caresses. It was as if he became a different person with her. Why was it that Masha was able to do this when nobody else even dared to try? For one of us to have done it would have seemed unnatural, while she was simple and sincere. I do not mean to say that the rest of us loved him less—not at all—only that the expression of love was not as warm and natural as it was with her. (p. 241)

A lifelong wanting to get parental approval and admiration even if it is in vain may be thought of as a parental spur to creative contributions. In 1943, the *New Yorker* magazine ran a profile of Gilbert Grosvenor, editor and founder of the *National Geographic* magazine. Grosvenor wrote *New Yorker* editor Harold Ross a courtly letter of thanks for "the honor you have done me and the *National Geographic* magazine." A somewhat stunned Ross wrote him back saying "the *National Geographic* was my father's favorite magazine. . . . If he were alive, I'd show him your letter to impress him as I never was able to impress him during his lifetime" (quoted from *National Geographic* magazine).

In Part I, Robert Bly's words convey profound, thoughtful, sometimes mischievous, often spiritual and vulnerable truths. His poetry, singing, and lectures have made him one of the most important contemporary poets. He is widely known for his workshops and lectures on men and on fathers. His own father was an alcoholic and his mother treated him as "a special person," wounding him in another way, but while he knew the dark shadow side of human nature, it is the hopeful spirit of humanity which he conveys.

Elisabeth Kübler-Ross has a capacity for empathy and the giving of unconditional love to heal parents and children who are dying. When I asked her to talk in Salado on the theme "My Mother, My Father," she replied that she would talk, but on the subject of "Life, Death and Transition." She did not want to talk about her mother and father. I was therefore astonished and moved when she stood up at the lectern to deliver her address and began telling us about her mother and father. For the first time I understood Elisabeth Kübler-Ross and her dedication to healing and caring for dying children who could not say what they wished about death and about their inner world because parents didn't know how to let them do it. Kübler-Ross's message is inspiring as she conveys the potential for goodness in each of us beyond our imagination, a giving which seeks no reward, a listening without judgment, and loving unconditionally. And like Robert Bly, she knows how to face the shadow or the dark side of our goodness.

Mary Catherine Bateson's book, *With a Daughter's Eye: A Memoir of Margaret Mead and Gregory Bateson*, was featured on the front page of the *New York Times* Book Review (August 26, 1984) under the headline, "Views of a Culture Heroine." I had heard her mother lecture, and her father, Gregory Bateson, was a friend of mine who lived a block from me when I lived in California. He wrote a chapter in my book, *Social Psychiatry in Action*. He had a profound effect upon me. Mary Catherine Bateson wrote, "Through my mother's writing echoes the question, 'What kind of world can we *build* for our children?' " and "Once in my childhood, Ray Birdwhistell said to me, 'Your mother has such a masculine mind and your father such a feminine mind.' I bridled, for this was in the fifties when a comment like that seemed to be a disparagement of Gregory. Margaret in those days was already a celebrity to the general public, while almost no one outside a small circle of anthropologists and psychotherapists knew who Gregory was. People asked me, 'How does it feel to have such a famous mother?' and would go on to say, 'and what does your father do?' Ray then continued, 'Margaret is always shooting thousands of ideas out in all directions, like sperm, while Gregory, when he has an idea, he sits on it, and develops it like a big ovum.' " Mary Catherine Bateson has much to tell us of the uniqueness of having two famous parents and ways in which subjectivity, disciplined and brought to consciousness, contributes to knowledge.

Jerome Kagan's chapter is a solid challenge to many psychological principles entrenched in clinical practice and our culture: that early childhood deprivations will mark the child for later emotional and developmental problems. He does not argue that parent–child bonds do not matter, but that many aspects of parenting are not so crucial as we think. He presents evidence to suggest that the customary concepts of developmental stages are not correct. The *New York Times* book reviewer of Kagan's volume, *The Nature of the Child*, had once been a student of Kagan's in 1971, and he recalls the excitement at Harvard when Kagan told a group of colleagues and students some startling results of his research project in Guatemala. The Mayan Indians of northwest Guatemala swaddled their infants in pieces of cloth and left them suspended in hammocks in the darkness of their houses for many hours of the day. Yet, despite spending much of their earliest years hanging in a dark room, by later childhood these same children were as alert and psychologically developed as children from other cultures who spend these hours of infancy in what we think of as a more beneficial manner.

Are Kagan's findings related to the Ilya Tolstoy's life? Do these findings help clarify Mary Catherine Bateson's story? Have we become true believers of our convictions of how to raise children?

Jerome Kagan and I had dinner before his Salado lecture and he said to me, "You don't necessarily have to *know* the person who might have greatly influenced your life. The person who influenced me the most was my grandfather. I never knew him. He died before I was born. But my mother always talked to me about him. She told me that he was a scholar. In fact, she said that when he died he had a book on his chest." There was a long silence. Then I urged him to develop this idea in his lecture. He didn't. I suppose a real scientist doesn't talk about what he knows at the same time as about what he doesn't know. Kagan's chapter on "The Power and Limitations of Parents" follows Betty Sue Flowers short essay originally titled "Heroic Women" but changed to "Powerful Women: Mother, Grandmother, Great Grandmother." The generations of mothers and power are variations of the theme of Mary Catherine Bateson's story of a culture heroine. Flowers' chapter is an elaboration of comments she made at the Salado Institute's symposium, "Texas Myths: The Personal and the Collective Mythology."

Part II focuses on the nonpersonal mother and father with ramifications in mythology, religion, history, and Jungian psychology. Elizabeth Silverthorne's chapter on Mariolatry in art fits into the evolving messages of this book, in the light of mother and infant, the eternal woman, and the Christian symbolism and meaning of Mary, the Mother of Christ. The virgin mother is also a myth associated with the goddesses. Silverthorne is writing about Our Mother in Heaven.

Mary Briner, an American Jungian analyst, has lived in Switzerland for many years. She is a famous teacher of Jungian psychology at the C. G. Jung Institute. Many years ago she gave me a copy of her seminars on Mother–Daughter Relationship at the Zürich Institute. She is continuing to give these clinical seminars, developing and changing them. When I last saw her in Switzerland, I asked her if she would let us publish her latest revision of her mother and daughter seminars. At first she was completely opposed to the idea because of the personal nature of the material. But I told her that it was possible to remove revealing personal aspects of life histories of patients in a way which would help others throughout the world. Mary Briner hesitated because she never published papers or clinical reports, but in the end she agreed, much to the benefit of our readers.

John Silber's chapter on the "Myth of the Hero" builds up to the fathers and the myth's implication in our political, social, and cultural history. Silber's essay was originally delivered as the keynote address at the Salado Institute's symposium, "Texas Myth: The Personal and the Collective Mythology." Dr. Silber, a Texan, now president of Boston University, widely known and respected as a scholar and a university president, outspoken in controversy, is eminently qualified to speak of the myth of the hero. He understands collective and personal psychology as an historian and creator of bold ideas that affect the education of children from elementary schools through universities.

The last two chapters relating to Jung and his father were delivered at the National Conference of Jungian Analysts, New York, May 1984. Murray Stein's chapter reflects on the idea of the significance of Jung's father in his destiny as a therapist of Christianity.

The final chapter by myself was written as a response to Murray Stein's paper. I was asked at the last moment to take the place of the assigned respondent who was unable to attend the meeting. I look at Jung, the father–son relationship, but do not address the issue of the idea of Jung as therapist to Christianity. I suggest a point of view at variance with the traditional view of Jung and his father. I sent a copy of my talk to Jung's son, Franz, who lives in Kusnacht and is a friend of mine. He wrote back and said, "You are right, especially when one has in mind that very few materials, for instance, no letters between father and son and vice versa, are published. To judge just out of the 'Memories, Dreams, and Reflections,' is a bit too simple. I like your opposition and the remark: 'There was a gentle carrying of son and of father; Paul and Carl, Carl and Paul,' etc. is absolutely right." (Published with permission.)

I have brought personal memories of my father into my chapter. I can objectively understand father and son only to a point. Then, as Mary Catherine Bateson said, "subjectivity, disciplined and brought to consciousness, contributes to knowledge."

One day when I was writing this introduction I looked up at the photograph of my father which he gave me when I was 14 years old. He had inscribed on it, "Live to serve. Then you will live forever, and I will not have lived in vain. Devotedly your dad, Harry A. Wilmer." What an elegant sentiment, and yet an admonition with a heavy burden on a son, to follow his father's precepts so he will live forever and his father's life will not have been in vain. And what does it mean to "Live to serve?" This inscription moved me but troubled me.

Thinking about this, I recalled another such comment he had given to me when I was 12 years old. He had printed on a card which he gave to me on January 7, 1929, just 60 years ago:

> And when all your tasks are done,
> I hope the world will be much better
> Because you have lived my son.

I have no trouble with that and I think that each of the contributors to this book might be living under just such a guiding spirit.

Harry A. Wilmer

PART I

MY MOTHER
MY FATHER

CHAPTER ONE

Father and Son

Robert Bly

Adapted from the lecture and discussion entitled "Thoughts on Fathers and Sons," presented at the Institute for the Humanities at Salado, November 17, 1985.

About Robert Bly

Robert Bly spends much of the year in his quiet hometown of Moose Lake, Minnesota, with his wife and family. In addition to being a poet, critic, editor, publisher, translator, musician, and political activist, he is widely sought after as a speaker and teacher.

On November 17, 1985, Bly explored the subject of "Fathers and Sons" with the members of the Institute for the Humanities at Salado by talking, singing, and reading his poetry as he accompanied himself on a dulcimer. He mentioned that it was only a few years earlier that he realized he was not as close to his father as he was to his mother and never had been. Knowing that time was growing short, he consciously tried to change that relationship.

Bly received his undergraduate degree from Harvard in 1950 and his masters from the University of Iowa in 1956. He was awarded a grant by the Fulbright Foundation and has been an Amy Lowell Fellow, a Rockefeller Foundation Fellow, and twice a Guggenheim Fellow. In 1968 he won the National Book Award in Poetry for *The Light Around the Body.*

He has translated 15 books from other languages and written 15 himself, including: *Silence in the Snowy Fields* (Middleton, Conn.: Wesleyan University Press, 1962); *The Man in the Black Coat Turns* (New York: Viking-Penguin, 1983); *Loving a Woman in Two Worlds* (New York: Dial, 1985); *News of the Universe: Poems of Twofold Consciousness* (San Francisco: Sierra Club, 1980); *Talking All Morning: Interviews about Politics and Poetry* (Ann Arbor, Mich.: University of Michigan Press, 1980); *Selected Poems:* (New York: Harper and Row, 1986); and *Iron John: A Book About Men* (forthcoming). The last book is an outgrowth of the workshops and talks he has conducted for men.

I

This paper concerns fathers—fathers and sons. And to a lesser extent, fathers and daughters. Most men and women would agree that the mother in our culture possesses a very powerful force field, and that in America the son remains in that force field—no blame to him or to his mother—for many years. I've found that a man usually doesn't begin to turn toward his father until he is about 45 years old. At the age of 40 to 45, a son begins to return to his father, to reperceive his father or brood about his father or long for a closer friendship. They've had years of separation.

In ancient life, when male initiation still guided the lives of men, a boy lived exclusively with his mother up to age nine or ten, when the initiating males arrived to take him away to a male enclosure. One could say that his separation from his father ended at this age. The pattern of father-and-son association set in the agricultural centuries amounted to constant labor close to one another, although there was often much emotional distance. The Industrial Revolution established a new pattern, one in which the father worked miles away from his son. (When I grew up as a farm boy in western Minnesota, I lived somewhere in between these two patterns. I worked with my father most of the summer days and for part of fall and spring, and saw him at work through all the seasons of the year. During the school year I went back to the farm when school was out and worked again in some association with him.) In the Industrial Revolution pattern, the father leaves the house to work and the parent remaining in the house is the mother. In this pattern, it is her values that usually fill the house. Women's values are marvelous; men's values, also marvelous, are different.

Being a parent could be described as a passing of values. It's clear that mothers are doing better in passing values on to their daughters today than fathers are in passing values on to their sons. I believe that values are passed when two bodies stand close to each other, whether they talk or not. A woman still spends many hours standing or working a few feet from her daughter. The average father in the United States today, according to the sociologists, spends ten minutes a day talking to his son, and he may not be standing close to him during those ten minutes.

In our culture then, very few positive male values get passed on to the sons in this bodily way. Speaking metaphorically, one could say that the father loses his son five minutes after birth.

The following is a prose poem which I wrote a few years ago, at a time when I first began to be aware of these things. This poem is called "Finding the Father."

This body offers to carry us for nothing—as the ocean carries logs—so on some days the body wails with its great energy, it smashes up the boulders, lifting small crabs, that flow around the sides. Someone knocks on the door, we do not have time to dress. He wants us to come with him through the blowing and rainy streets, to the dark house. We will go there, the body says, and there find the father whom we have never met, who wandered in a snowstorm the night we were born, who then lost his memory, and has lived since longing for his child, whom he saw only once . . . while he worked as a shoemaker, as a cattle herder in Australia, as a restaurant cook who painted at night. When you light the lamp you will see him. He sits there behind the door . . . the eyebrows so heavy, the forehead so light . . . lonely in his whole body, waiting for you.

When the father lives his primary life away from the house, the mother often lacks a resonating box, if we might describe it so, where her longing for close relationship with a man can resonate. She may then choose her son. When this happens, the son receives the intensity that should better be absorbed by a man the mother's own age, and this incoming intensity, using his body as a resonator, seems a burden to him as well as a secret pleasure. A sort of conspiracy develops, conducted in secret as true conspiracies are, and the two conspirators—mother and son—push the father away still further . . . "behind the door" as the poem describes it.

The son receives psychic heat, flattery, attention, support, and "specialness" for his part in this conspiracy; but he also becomes elevated to an adult, even godlike, status too early. Through being a god he can lose contact with his father, and in fact with the whole human world. I described the part I played in such a conspiracy in a poem called "Fifty Males Sitting Together."

After a long walk in the woods clear cut for lumber,
lit up by a few young pines,
I turn home,
drawn to water. A coffinlike band
softens half the lake,
draws the shadow
down from westward hills.
It is a massive
masculine shadow,
fifty males sitting together
in hall or crowded room,
lifting something indistinct
up into the resonating night.

Sunlight kindles the water still free of shadow,
kindles it till it glows with the high
pink of wounds.
Reeds stand about in groups
unevenly as if they might
finally ascend
to the sky all together.
Reeds protect
the band near shore.
Each reed has its own thin
thread of darkness inside;
it is relaxed and rooted in the black
mud and snail shells under the sand.

The woman stays in the kitchen, and does not want
to waste fuel by lighting a lamp,
as she waits
for the drunk husband to come home.
Then she serves him
food in silence.
What does the son do?
He turns away,
loses courage,
goes outdoors to feed with wild
things, lives among dens
and huts, eats distance and silence;
he grows long wings, enters the spiral, ascends.

How far he is from working men when he is forty!
From all men! The males singing
chant far out
on the water grounded in downward shadow.
He cannot go there because
he has not grieved
as humans grieve. If someone's
head was cut
off, whose was it?
The father's? Or the mother's? Or his?
The dark comes down slowly, the way
snow falls, or herds pass a cave mouth.
I look up at the other shore; it is night.

How can such a conspiracy be broken? I don't believe the father can
effectively break it . . . he is the outsider, the one *without* power. The
mother or the son must break it. But why should they? The following story
tells of a mother who decided she didn't want the conspiracy any longer.

I was asked a few years ago by the C. G. Jung Institute of Chicago to give a talk on the initiation of males. About three-fourths of the audience were women. I mentioned that the ancients believed that a woman could change the sperm to a boy, but could not change the boy to a man. That had to be done by other men. Some women grew furious; others considered the idea sensible. One of these remarked that when her son reached high-school age, she knew he needed something "harder" than she could give him; but she found that if she tried to provide that hardness, she lost her own feminine side; she found herself in a dilemma. Several women mentioned how attractive the "conspiracy" was, particularly if no adult males were in the house, and several found the conspiracy attractive even while the husband was living in the house. One woman told this story.

> I had two teenage boys. My husband and I usually went together each year to San Francisco for a conference. But this time I had just returned from a Jungian retreat for women—my first. I was in touch with an unlived part of my life, and I had a longing to be alone and think about it. So I said to my husband, "Instead of taking me to San Francisco, why don't you take the boys?" My husband looked a little wounded and said, "Do you mean you don't want to go with me?" I answered, "No, I think it would be good if you took the boys."
>
> So he took the boys, and as a result of the trip, something changed. The boys had never been alone with their father before, in a real sense. Of course they had cleaned the garage together or gone to games, but they hadn't been alone with their father for several days. This was something different. After they got back the boys insisted on a relationship with their father. They would say, "We want you to do this with us." That was a wonderful change for them.
>
> The next year when the conference came up, he took the boys again, and I went off to be alone. When they returned, I was in the kitchen. One of my boys—he was about 13 at the time—came up behind me where I was standing at the sink and put his arms around me. Without intending to, I suddenly threw my arms out, and my whole body leapt, and he bounced off the wall. When he stood up, our relationship was different.

This is an example of the mother intervening to break the conspiracy, although a close relationship with the father seems to have been essential in lessening the shock of this particular break.

How else can the conspiracy be broken? If the mother does not intervene decisively, then the son, after some years have passed, can move to do so. But many years, I feel, have to go by before he can do this. The old initiatory practices (such as the Hopis still follow) provide for an abrupt break with the mother sometime between the ages of eight and twelve. When the break is left to the son, he may be 40 or 50 years old before consciousness of the conspiracy becomes intense enough to enable him to break out of it.

The conspiracy between the mother and the son is more intense, I think, if the son is artistic. In our family my mother preferred me, the clean version, so to speak, to my father, the old, dirty version. I entered into that conspiracy before I could write my name. I was no doubt half conscious when I agreed, but not strong enough to refuse. I needed everything I could get. We can't blame the mother for this or ourselves either, but we can appreciate the father's dismay when he notices that his wife prefers his son to him. It's his own son, so what can he do about it? Nothing. And the conspiracy lasts a long time, because we, as sons, love that female attention.

Up until about ten years ago, I visited my parents quite often; they were still living on the farm. My father had had an operation for lung cancer and was often in bed. His bed was in the room right next to the living room. This was the typical scene: I arrived, visited with my mother in the living room for 30 minutes, and if I remembered, I said goodbye to my father before I left. Now how do you think my father felt hearing that talk out there?

A similar scene is that which occurs when children call their parents from college. The son or daughter gets their father on the phone, and he says, "I'll give you your mother." The father feels he doesn't have the right to talk. They want to talk to their mother, and he knows that. "I'll give you your mother. Here she is." Part of this is the reluctance of the American man to talk, and part of it is just the feeling, "I am out of it. Those two—the mother and son—have it. They're the ones. I used to have it, but I don't have it anymore. They have it now." We need to become conscious of this. It isn't necessary to shout at the mother and say, "I'm sick of this conspiracy. I don't even remember signing the paper!" That doesn't do any good because she can't remember signing it either. It's a fact of life in the house, like a leaking roof.

After I realized what was happening, I began to go in and sit down with my father on a chair next to the bed. We'd sit and talk. He was not a great conversationalist, but that was all right. After 15 or 20 minutes my mother would come in and sit down on the bed if she wanted to talk to me. That was fine. She would sit on the bed and all three of us would talk. I didn't have to say anything; everybody knew something had happened, that there was a change.

I recognized that my next job was to reperceive my father. A son or daughter will never get an accurate picture of the father from the mother. There is no blame in this, but it requires hard work.

II

I have discovered several things about my own father in attempting to reperceive him. I'll begin with a poem called "A Prodigal Son," whose subject is the difficulty we have looking into our parents' faces as they grow old. The man mentioned in the first stanza is a friend I had in high school. In the third stanza I refer to the old Hassidic tale about father–son relationships. This tale is only possible in a family that has been living in the same apartment for generations.

> The Prodigal Son is kneeling in the husks,
> He remembers the man about to die
> who cried, "Don't let me die, Doctor."
> The swine go on feeding in the sunlight.
>
> When he folds his hands, his knees on corncobs,
> he sees the smoke of ships
> floating off the isles of Tyre and Sidon,
> and father beyond father beyond father.
>
> An old man once, being dragged across the floor
> by his shouting son, cried:
> "Don't drag me any farther than that crack on the floor—
> I only dragged my father that far."
>
> My father is seventy-five years old.
> How difficult it is,
> bending the head, looking into the water
> Under the water there's a door the pigs have gone
>   through.

The image of the pigs going through the door is mysterious—to me also. A few years ago I wrote some reminiscences.

> I'll tell you a story about my father. Each year men from south of us—Kansas, Missouri, Arkansas, even Alabama and Tennesse— would move through the country following the small grain harvest north. They would end up in North Dakota or Canada about late September, and would then go home again. (This would be around 1940–1943, just before the war, when

people still used threshing rigs and the combine hadn't come in.) My father, since he ran a threshing rig, would hire one or two of these men each threshing season. Sometimes I went with him. At 6:00 a.m. before the rig had started, we would drive uptown to a small park, in which some of the men had slept the night. We'd drive around the park. And if he saw a man with a face he liked, he'd ask him if he could pitch bundles and drive a team of horses. And he had very good judgment on that, very good.

On one of these mornings he hired a man whom I will call Garth Morrison, who had come up from a small town in Missouri. Garth turned out to be a good worker, and he and my father got on together very well. He stayed with us during the week. On Saturday night, the teams put away, he would go to town and be gone Saturday and Sunday nights. But early Monday morning he would always be back and ready for work.

On one Monday morning he didn't show up. My father was puzzled. And about 9:00 a.m. he put someone else in charge of the rig and drove to town to see if he could find Garth. Asking around here and there, he heard that Garth had been picked up by the sheriff Saturday night. Apparently he had made a date with a waitress at the cafe, who had agreed to let him walk her home. At 11:00 he'd gone to pick her up, and probably to his surprise she did let him walk her home, where she lived with her parents. A few words were exchanged, probably a series of misunderstood signals between a Southern man and a Northern woman. And he slapped her face. She went inside the house, furious and complaining. Her parents called the sheriff. The man was from out of state. And the sheriff and the judge had a secret court session the next morning, Sunday morning, having refused all along to let Garth call my father on the telephone, and they sentenced him to 20 years at Stillwater Prison. By Sunday noon he was on his way to Stillwater already. By Sunday night the sheriff was back in town. And it was said that he always tried to show proof of his vigilance shortly before an election.

My father, once he got the story from the reluctant sheriff, was enraged. He shut down the threshing rig, and he drove a couple of miles and found his best friend Alvin. They got in the car and they drove to St. Paul, it was about three hours, and went to see the Attorney General. The Attorney General agreed that the facts gave off a very bad odor. And so he got in the car with my father and my father's best friend, and they drove to Stillwater Prison, which was about an hour and a half. And there they talked to Garth and verified the story. The Attorney General then had Garth taken out of prison and returned to the county jail in Madison, this little town, to await trial. He stayed in the county jail a month or more, and we as boys would go up and talk with him through the window, giving him doughnuts and stuff. And my father hired a lawyer and paid for Garth's wife and infant son to come up from Missouri for the trial. I remember him holding the baby on the stand. The jury convicted Garth of simple assault, and the judge ruled that the time already spent in jail more than served out the appropriate sentence. He was released, and his family returned to Missouri.

My father never spoke to the sheriff again for the rest of the sheriff's life. Garth did not come north again either. The spring following the trial Garth and his wife invited my father and mother down to Missouri for a visit. They drove down, and it turned out that everyone in that small Missouri town knew the story. When my father went to a restaurant there, no one would accept money from him.

This anecdote moved me very much, and I wrote this little comment at the end:

To be able to respect your father is such a beautiful thing. I learned then that the indignation of a solitary man is the stone pin that connects this world to the next.

The more easygoing businessmen in Madison, who had so many friends, would have left Garth sitting in his cell for 20 years. They would have been afraid to put their hand into the web of social transience, afraid the web wouldn't be repaired overnight, or the spider of loneliness would bite them. I learned too that when you've been unselfish, people respond not in words, but by feeding you. I learned so much in that one story. We don't need to read books on ethics or see documentaries on television. One moral example will do for a lifetime.

Next, I want to consider the other side of the father. We usually call this dark side "the shadow." The following is a poem called "Snow Geese" which mentions, as it begins, the Canadian geese that fly down through the Minnesota farm country in the fall on the way south, eating ears of corn knocked off by the picker.

The dark geese treading blowing Dakota snows
Over the fence stairs of the small farms come,
Slipping through cries flung up into the night,
And settling, ah, between them, shifting wings,
Light down at last in bare and snowy fields.

> The drunken father has pulled the boy inside.
> The boy breaks free, turns, leaves the house.
> He spends that night out eating with the geese
> Where, alert and balancing on wide feet,
> Crossing rows, they walk through the broken stalks.

Like many children of alcoholics, I left the house often. Other such children describe walking for hours on the railroad track, or walking in woods or in strange parts of town. The poem touches on the experience of exile, separation, eviction, accompanying some attempt to preserve feeling more honest than one sees in the house. This is not all bad, of course, because, as the poem says, exile put me in touch with the wild geese.

Having an alcoholic parent resembles, as someone has said, having an elephant in the living room that no one mentions. The hurricane mood that surrounds the alcoholic parent teaches the child that his or her moods are of no significance. The parent does what he wants to do and, in the terms of the next poem, shows all his teeth, while the child hides his. The next poem is called "My Father's Wedding: 1924." I began it one day while doing an exercise in object writing with some younger poets. A friend brought in a big stick from the woods behind his house. We put it on a table, and as I began to write about it, I noticed it was bent like a bad knee, and it seemed to be my father's wounded leg, the one I had never seen, his third invisible leg, so to speak.

> Today, lonely for my father, I saw
> a log, or branch,
> long, bent, ragged, bark gone.
> I felt lonely for my father when I saw it.
> It was the log
> that lay near my uncle's old milk wagon.
>
> Some men live with a limp they don't hide,
> stagger, or drag
> a leg. Their sons often are angry.
> Only recently I thought:
> Doing what you want . . .
> Is that like limping? Tracks of it show in sand.
>
> Have you seen those giant bird-
> men of Bhutan?
> Men in bird masks, with pig noses, dancing,
> teeth like a dog's, sometimes
> dancing on one bad leg!
> They do what they want, the dog's teeth say that.

But I grew up without dog's teeth,
showed a whole body,
left only clear tracks in sand.
I learned to walk swiftly, easily,
no trace of a limp.
I even leaped a little. Guess where my defect is!

Then what? If a man, cautious,
hides his limp,
somebody has to limp it. Things
do it; the surroundings limp.
House walls get scars,
the car breaks down; matter, in drudgery, takes it up.

On my father's wedding day,
no one was there
to hold him. Noble loneliness
held him. Since he never asked for pity
his friends thought he
was whole. Walking alone he could carry it.

He came in limping. It was a simple
wedding, three
or four people. The man in black,
lifting the book, called for order.
And the invisible bride
stepped forward, before his own bride.

He married the invisible bride, not his own.
In her left
breast she carried the three drops
that wound and kill. He already had
his bark-like skin, then,
made rough especially to repel the sympathy
he longed for, didn't need, and wouldn't accept.
So the Bible's
words are read. The man in black
speaks the sentence. When the service
is over, I hold him
in my arms for the first time and the last.

After that he was alone
and I was alone.
Few friends came; he invited few.
His two-story house he turned
into a forest,
where both he and I are the hunted.

What is the dark side of my father? He did what he wanted to do and so became a tornado in the house, something to which we all had to pay attention. I heard the metaphor recently: "A tornado respects no boundaries; it opens doors, collapses houses, lifts your bed and lets it fall, leaves the house owners feeling weak. All they can say is, 'I guess we'll rebuild.' "

What did I get from my father? I think the political work I've done has come from him. During the Vietnam War I took part in the protest against it, although I had never engaged in leftist action before. The example my father had set was important to me. When we take a moral stand, we don't know whether it's right or wrong or what. We have to do what we think. My father was willing to do what he did alone, without any support.

When I refused to go along with the Vietnam War, I felt myself closer to my father. It's a strange thing that those men who fought in the Vietnam War felt and feel themselves, for the most part, farther from their fathers. The war involved a failure of political intelligence and understanding, but also a failure of human planning in the field, and that was a failure that old men had more to do with than young men. One of the most terrible images I've ever seen was shown in a short film toward the end of the Vietnam War. Four or five men, sitting around a fire, had taken a rifle apart, put pot in the rifle barrel, and lit it. They were passing around the rifle barrel and sucking on the end of it. I've never forgotten it because it evoked the image of four young boys sucking on the nipple. In a way—terrifying. Were they not trying to get some comfort out of that pot? There were only young men out there, abandoned by the older men.

I have a certain pride in men, and that comes from watching my father as he talked and worked with men. Some respect or honor he had for his father seemed to carry over into his relationship with every farmer or farmhand with whom he dealt. He treated each man as someone capable of breaking and took care not to invade their private wound or damage their self-esteem.

In our house my father had a certain sort of sovereignty of opinions. When my brother and I were about 15, he bought us a 1940 Ford, a beautiful little black coupe. Several women stopped him on the street at that time and said, "Jacob, you shouldn't do this. You have two nice boys there, and you're going to ruin them. They're going to end up chasing women in neighboring towns" (which was true) "and it will be your fault." My father didn't answer. He turned and walked away. He had made up his own mind and he rested with his opinion, right or wrong. The story may also suggest some lack of respect for women and their perceptions, and that is a part of his dark side.

James Hillman recently remarked that both Freud and Jung were mother's men, and that this has thrown psychology off from the beginning. Freud pays little attention to the father as a positive force in the son's life, as a source and object of longing. My experience with men's retreats suggests otherwise. We often begin with the mother–son relationship and stories of the mother's power, conscious and unconscious, and this information is met with interest and varying degrees of fear. But when we move later to the father, when men go into their longing for the father, the grief becomes so deep that the mother days fade and are forgotten. The longing for the father, the distant father, and the memories of what he did and didn't do, resonate so deeply in the psyche that grief wells up. "And you my father there on that sad height." We need to realize that when we turn toward the father, half of the men or more will end up weeping.

III

How can we escape this pain over the remote or untalkative father? Escape this sorrow over a father who did what he wanted and thereby took away the wishes, or ability to wish, of his wife and children? How can we stop feeling sorry for ourselves once we see what happened? Who imagines that anyone can receive from an aged father what he did not receive when his father was young and vigorous? For many of us, men and women, these are serious questions.

In Africa, when a serious question comes up, someone is sure to say, "I'll tell you a story." I will tell you one now. It's an African story about father and son.

> A father and son went out hunting one morning. Soon the father killed a rat, a wood rat, and gave it to the son to keep. But the son thought it of no significance and threw it in the bush. As it happens, they found no more game that day. On some days one catches only rats. So toward evening the father said, "Give me that rat, so that we may cook it, and we will have something to eat." The son said, "I threw it in the bush." The father in his rage took up his axe, hit the boy, and the boy fell unconscious. The father left. After a while the son woke up, walked back to his village, where everyone was asleep, walked into his mother and father's hut, took his clothes, and left, walking on a dark path toward the forest.

This story is meant to evoke personal memory in us. When did I get that axe blow from my father? And fall unconscious? When did he walk away? The story suggests that the father didn't even wait to see if his son—or daughter—was still alive.

Some men, when they've heard the story, feel that axe blow intensely. They are the boy in the story and know instantly where the blow fell. Most of them feel it on the head, but others feel the blow on their left side, or in the stomach, or on the back, or in the groin. And the injustice of it evokes rage. It's true, of course, that in the story the son gives the first blow. If we imagine the rat as the father's occupation, then most of us have metaphorically given our fathers a solid blow by throwing away his occupation. And yet I don't think any of us do wrong in throwing away our father's rat. But one blow usually produces another.

How can we be initiated by a man who has given us a blow of that severity? We probably can't. It is a truism in ancient life that the father does not initiate his son—the initiation is done by unrelated older males. Only these old men—not closely related—can lead the boy into the spirit.

The implication is that we must not expect too much from our fathers. The story says that at one point you'll walk to your mother and father's house and while they are asleep take your clothes and leave, "walking down a long road in the dark." A son then needs a second father, or an older helpful man, who will guide him beyond the point where his father could take him. The son needs to look for such a mentor consciously, in the way young painters in the Middle Ages traveled weeks to put themselves under the tutelage of a mentor. The mentoring concept falters in the mass university system we have today, and this is a problem.

To continue with the African story:

> After walking a long way down the road in the dark, the boy came to another village. Everyone in that village was asleep, except the Chief, whose hut stood in the center of the village and was lighted. The boy went to the door, and the Chief said, "How is it with you?" The boy said, "My father and I went hunting this morning. He killed a rat and gave it to me to keep, but I thought it of no significance and threw it into the bush. Toward sundown he asked me for the rat, and I said, "I threw it in the bush." Then my father took his axe and hit me, and I fell down unconscious. Later I woke up and I went to my mother and father's hut in the night and took my clothes, and walked down the road through the forest and came here. That's how it is with me."

You can see that he told the story clearly; apparently that clarity is necessary before the next thing can happen. The chief now says, "Can you keep a secret?" The boy says, "What secret?" The chief says, "I had a son who was killed in battle. Will you be my son? Can you keep that secret?" The boy says, "Yes."

The story goes on from there, and eventually the boy is asked to choose between the two fathers. The early part of the story declares with great visual power that sooner or later we will have to leave our father, and that after a long walk in the dark, we may find another father, who is described here as a chief, or a "lion-king." The second father leads a son (it is not necessarily different with a daughter, but this particular story is about a son) into spiritual knowledge or spiritual disciplines to which the physical father has not brought him.

There is a tradition in early Christianity that several Gospels existed beyond the four that we know. A fifth Gospel called the Gospel of Thomas has been translated and published recently. It was first found in 1947 and is a collection of 121 sayings of Jesus, which I think are genuine. The first saying goes this way. "So you think the kingdom of the spirit is in the sea, do you? Well then the fishes will get there before you. You think the kingdom of the spirit is in the sky? Then the birds will get there before you. But it is not there—it is inside and outside at the same second." This is a very subtle idea.

If you read the literature surrounding King Arthur and others from the Middle Ages, you find that in the twelfth, thirteenth, and fourteenth centuries, when a young boy reached the age of 12 or so, he was sent into "fosterage." As a father, this meant you chose an uncle or an older good friend of yours and you sent your boy to him. Thus at 12 years old, the son left his mother and was sent to an older male who taught him.

Those of you familiar with Grimms' tale, "Iron John" or "Iron Hans," know that the eight-year-old boy in it eventually goes with Iron John or the Wild Man to the sacred pond in the forest to receive instruction. This Wild Man can be seen as a second father, or lion-king. But in our culture there is considerable confusion between the Wild Man and the Savage Man. The Wild Man stands for spontaneity preserved from childhood, for a union with nature, for a positive image of male sexuality, for Zen priests and such initiators into the spirit, and finally for a male divinity many thousands of years old. We see the Savage Man in Hell's Angels motorcyclists, in Clint Eastwood, and in popular media figures such as Rambo. A man I met on a plane once remarked that every European city he had visited one summer had a Rambo movie showing. The United States is guilty of making and exporting these movies, which present an alternate father who has none of the radiance and grief of the African lion-king. Rambo does not provide a fruitful, human way out of the dilemma of the unfeeling or untalkative father.

IV

I used an old Chinese poem written by Tao Yuan-Ming as an epigraph for one of my own books of poems.

> After a storm the leafy tree is no longer solid,
> but the pine still throws a full shadow.
> It has found a place to be.
> For a thousand years it will not give up this place.

I understand the poem to say that when a man or woman tries to see what actually happened in his or her family, and goes into the grief voluntarily—eats the grief, so to speak—he or she slowly changes from a leafy tree, which a wind can strip of leaves, to a pine tree. Solidity and strength enter.

I don't think that the work men do, or men's mythology, or investigation of father-and-son sorrow brings them to a place more distant from women. On the contrary, I think it brings them closer. When men work, they become more rooted, less open to destructive storms, more able to hold their ground. When women work, they also become more rooted, less open to destructive storms, more able to hold their ground.

As for our mothers and fathers, we will never know their lives or their souls. I'll close with this brief poem about sitting against a pine tree.

> After writing poems all day,
> I went off to see the moon on the piney hill.
> Far in the woods I sit down against a pine.
> The moon has her porches turned to face the light,
> but the deep part of her house is in darkness.

CHAPTER TWO

On Being Born, On Caring and On Dying

Elisabeth Kübler-Ross

Adapted from a lecture and discussion entitled "Life, Death and Transition," presented at the Institute for the Humanities at Salado, November 3, 1985.

About Elisabeth Kübler-Ross

Elisabeth Kübler-Ross believes that each one of us has the potential for loving unconditionally. The goal of the Elisabeth Kübler-Ross Center and Shanti Niyala, a nonprofit organization now located in the Shenandoah Valley near Head Waters, Virginia, is to help as many individuals as possible to reach that potential. On November 3, 1985, Dr. Kübler-Ross spoke to Institute members about her background, her views on life and death, and her work with the terminally ill (especially children) and those who love them.

Swiss-born Kübler-Ross is a world-famous lecturer and author. But as one of a set of triplets, with an identical sister, she grew up searching for an identity of her own. This background, plus the horror and devastation of Europe after the Second World War, led her into medicine and finally to the field of psychiatry. Her compassionate and sensitive work with the terminally ill of all ages created the demand that she share her insight and understanding of their feelings and needs. This she has done through her lectures, writing, workshops, and training programs.

Dr. Kübler-Ross, who graduated from the University of Zurich with an M.D. in 1957, is a naturalized American citizen. She was a resident in psychiatry at Montefiore Hospital in New York and at the University of Colorado Medical School. Awarded honorary degrees by 19 American universities and colleges, including Notre Dame, Loyola, Amherst, Smith, and the University of Miami, she has held numerous teaching positions and served on numerous advisory boards. In 1979, *The Ladies Home Journal* named her Woman of the Decade, in 1980 she was given the Gold Plate Award of the American Academy of Achievement, and in 1981 she received the Teilhard prize. She is a founding member of the American Holistic Medical Association.

Her books include: *On Death and Dying* (New York: Macmillan, 1969); *Questions and Answers on Death and Dying* (New York: Macmillan, 1974); *Death—The Final Stage of Growth* (Englewood Cliffs, N.J.: Prentice-Hall, 1975); *To Live Until We Say Goodbye* (Englewood Cliffs, N.J.: Prentice-Hall, 1978); *Working It Through* (New York: Macmillan, 1982); *Living with Death and Dying* (New York: Macmillan, 1981); *Remember the Secret* (Berkeley, Calif.: Celestial Arts, 1982); *On Children and Death* (New York: Macmillan, 1983); and *AIDS: The Ultimate Challenge* (New York: Macmillan, 1987).

I will start with my own father and mother. You'll probably think back about your own life experiences, not just what you remember about your father and mother, but what you were told about when you were born. That sets the tone for the rest of your life. You should not tell children too many horror stories, because it's good when you forget the nightmares of your birth. It is not wise to add unnecessary burdens.

The story I heard about when I was born was that my parents wanted a baby girl very, very badly. They had a six-year-old son who was the crown prince and spoiled as could be. They thought it was time to have a daughter. As my mother grew bigger and bigger, their expectations grew bigger and bigger. This daughter was to be gorgeous, with lots of hair, and she had to be pretty and she had to be chubby. When I was born, I was an absolute disaster. I was the ugliest shrink imaginable. I was less than two pounds, and a two-pound baby looks like a wet rat. In very vivid terms, they described their horrible disappointment in me. My mother had grown big with the pregnancy, and she was a small woman. The only excuse for this, which came 15 minutes later, was my sister. Totally unexpected, my twin, also two pounds, somewhat excused my being so tiny and so ugly. My mother kept saying, "There is more to come." My father said, "You have a problem," and the doctor, too, told my mother she had a problem. That was the first lesson I learned: when grown-ups don't want to face the grim reality, they blame it on others— on mothers, most of the time, but they always blame it on others. They cannot acknowledge that it might be true. To make a long story short, half an hour later, a six-and-a-half pound baby was born. And then the doctor and my father had to drop their denial. This story I heard over and over again. So the first lesson I learned in life, not by memory but by hearsay, was that grown-ups who don't want to face grim reality either put their heads in the sand or blame somebody else for it.

The second lesson I learned, which was very hard to live with, is that grown-ups are not honest. You all know, deep down inside, that you are not honest. You try to be honest, but you're really not. Remember back when an aunt called up and invited herself for dinner and you were sweet as you could be: "Oh, Aunt Rose, we are so looking forward to your coming." Then when you hung up the phone you said, "Harumph, why does she have to ruin our evening again with chatting all night?" You said all sorts of horrible things, while a three-year-old child stood behind you listening. Then when the doorbell rang and the aunt came in, the child said, "Why do you have to come again and ruin our evening?" What did you do? You smacked him and sent him to his bedroom and told him not to be so rude.

It is very hard for children to become honest, because we are not honest. We put on a nice face, but sometimes the truth slips out, and the children hear that. This is what they learn, for they learn from our behavior rather than the words we say on the telephone.

Parents are expected to know their children. But my parents did not know us, and they were not honest about it. They did not know which one was Elisabeth and which one was Erica. They had absolutely no idea. We have hundreds of photographs, and I don't know whether they are of me or my sister. In the old days, and I'm almost 60 now, they used to dress twins and triplets in identical dresses, socks, shoes, ribbons, and everything. This is a nightmare. It is show business. My parents never knew which child they were talking to. How can I be sure I'm not my sister standing here?

So what happened (because you are not supposed to not know your child)? They used combination names. Each time they were unsure, they gave us a combination name, one-half of my sister's name and one-half of my name. And each time they used a combination name I knew they didn't know to whom they spoke. Children are much smarter than we give them credit for being. So we learned very early that we could get away with murder, because they never knew which one to spank, which one to punish, or which one was a sweetie pie and which one a monster. I was the monster most of the time. My sister was very much more placid and more timid, but we tried everything we could think of to force grown-ups to recognize our individuality.

When we went to school, we hoped desperately that the teachers would be honest. They knew us as the famous Kübler triplets. My father was so thrifty that he gave all of us the same first initial, so that when dowry time came, he would have to make only one initial. This is typically Swiss. I still resent it that everybody was an "E"; my brother's name started with "E," and all three of us married someone whose name began with an "E." In a way, it is pathetic.

In school we tried to be very bad or very good, in order to have our own identity. We really deserved A's and F's. But the teachers wanted to be honest so they gave us straight C's. It was tragic for us children. Now it seems funny, looking back, but as children it told us that nobody really cared, that it didn't make any difference to them how it affected one to work so hard to deserve an A and end up with a C. You worked equally hard to deserve an F, and you still ended up with a C. It meant that only the outside is important.

When we became teenagers, things were not much better. My sister fell in love for the first time, and for teenagers the first love is the most important: she was really in love. The second time her boyfriend invited her out, my sister became very, very sick. We didn't know how sick at the time, but she was physically unable to go on that date. I said, in character, "If you really can't go, I'll go for you. He will never know the difference." We really went out on the thinnest branches hoping that somebody would know the difference. I asked her also how far she went, and that is another part of this honesty. I don't mean how far geographically. In Switzerland, to kiss somebody is going far. I went on that date for her, and when I came home I realized that her boyfriend had no idea he had gone out with her sister.

This marked my first conscious awareness that while we had absolutely everything in material terms—very loving, caring parents, a nice brother, siblings, pretty clothes, gorgeous house, beautiful garden—we had absolutely nothing. I could have dropped dead and nobody would have known; it was like being a clone. You cannot live without love. You can have millions of dollars, but if you don't have one human being who cares about you, not what you look like or how you talk or what you have, but you as an individual human being, it is worse than having nothing. It is absolutely impossible to live this way. Looking back, I can bless this upbringing, because it taught me early in life how to work with people who basically have everything but have nothing.

The day I became famous, November 21, 1969, when the *Life* magazine article came out, my life changed overnight. I went from being totally unknown to appearing in every magazine. That day, a friend of my mother's came to her and said, "Aren't you proud? Did you see the article?" And Mother said, "Uh huh." The friend continued, "Not one of your daughters, but two of your daughters are in the same issue." My identical triplet sister became famous overnight on the same day, in the same magazine. I was a few pages further back, but since my sister was married, nobody knew that we were the identical triplet sisters.

Do you understand what that does to a person? You try very hard to find out who you are, but there are some common links that go through a whole life naturally. You can learn to live with it if you find your own identity. In order to do that, I did relief work in Poland, Germany, and all over Europe, starting on the day in 1945, when the war ended. For the first time in my life, I discovered what real life was really about. Not doll clothes and nice smiles and pretty dresses, but what man does to his fellow man. In Switzerland there were no windstorms, there was no poverty, no unemployment, no war for 760 years. To be raised in Switzerland at the time when I was raised was not to be tested. If everything is sweet and loving and dandy and rich, there are never any windstorms. I always say that life has to put you through the tumbler a few times. And your choice is whether you come out crashed or polished.

I had never gone through a tumbler, and then I went through postwar Europe. It was a nightmare. It was hunger, and it was whole cities destroyed. I went to Majdanek, the concentration camp, where 960,000 children were killed. One can read Anne Frank, and one may even cry a few tears. But it is different to stand in front of the gas chambers, smelling the smell and seeing trainloads of baby shoes of murdered children. Can you grasp what that did to a 19-year-old Swiss girl? We had heard that there were concentration camps, but we never really understood what that meant. Now we saw trainloads of women's hair that had been removed from the victims to be shipped back to make cloth for winter coats. What this did to me was not only to open my eyes, but to make me wonder how men and women, mothers and fathers, could kill 960,000 children and the same day worry about their own child at home with chicken pox. In my search, in my exploration of how these children died, I went to the wooden barracks. There I saw little butterflies scratched into the wooden walls all over the concentration camp. At that time I had no idea what the butterflies meant.

While I looked at all this, I was absolutely speechless in the face of what man had done to his fellow man in the twentieth century. A young Jewish girl who stood there said, "You would be capable of doing that, too." And my first reaction was "No, no, absolutely not." I thought of Pestalozzi, our Swiss folk hero, who started the first orphanages in the world. I wanted to say, "I am not capable of that, I'm much more like Pestalozzi." But I could not say it because I realized that it's very easy to be loving in a positive environment. God knows what I would have become like if I had been raised in Nazi Germany. You can't judge if you have not been there.

So I didn't say anything. And she said, "There is a Hitler in all of us." If we became honest again like children, then we could acknowledge our negative side. I use that symbolically, our "Hitler." We can get rid of our Hitlers and we can all become Mother Theresas.

Three days later I was tested. I hitchhiked back through Germany to Switzerland with no food in my stomach. I mean nothing. Absolutely nothing. I suddenly realized that if a child walked by me with a piece of bread in her hands, I would be able to steal that piece of bread out of that child's hands. There is a beautiful Native American saying, "Don't judge your fellowman until you have walked in his moccasins for a mile."

I went back home and studied medicine. I became a physician, researcher, and scientist, and a very wishy-washy Protestant. This is my background. I'm glad this was my background, because I came to my research objectively. In the beginning I must admit I didn't have the slightest idea of what death was all about. We worked with many dying patients, and I observed clinically, very empirically. In my earliest book I described the stages of dying: you go through denial, then anger, then bargaining with God, then depression, and then, if you can really shed your tears and express your anger and nobody puts a Band-Aid on you, then you probably can die with acceptance. Acceptance doesn't mean you're happy, but it means that you can accept it. If you cannot express your tears and you cannot express your anger, then you die with resignation: "What's the use?" A lot of elderly people die this way.

Interestingly, many people who read my very earliest books, those written in 1968 or 1969, and read about those stages, now misuse them as five more labels. They stand in the doorway and if the patient is very angry, they don't talk to the patient—they go to the chart and write, "The patient is in a state of anger." This is ridiculous. Maybe the food is lousy and they should talk to the dietician! These guidelines must not be used just to give patients more labels. To die with dignity does not mean to die with peace and acceptance. It means to be allowed to die in character. If you have been a rebel and angry all your life, the likelihood that you rebel until you die is very high. Unconditional love means you accept your fellow man even when he's not where you want him to be.

In my clinical observations I saw that even the people who gave nurses a hard time and called the doctor frequently and complained about everything, the moment after they died, had an incredible peaceful expression on their faces. They were nasty all their lives and now they had this peaceful expression on their faces. This triggered my curiosity and began my quest to find an answer.

In the 1960s medicine changed, drastically and horribly. Remember that I had been a country doctor in Switzerland, which was very different from being a doctor in a university hospital in the United States. In my practice in the country, I had seven villages all by myself. I sat the whole night with a child who had a high fever until the fever was broken. I ate a lot of pies, I had a lot of cigarettes and coffee.

In the 1960s when the transplants began, our nightmare started. We got lawsuits charging that, for example, we had used a kidney from a patient who was not dead. There were accidents where both husband and wife were killed, and we were forced to ascertain which one died two minutes earlier because of last wills, money matters, material things. A minister and I who worked together as a team in death-and-dying seminars had a hard time because physicians who had been helping, caring professionals were suddenly worried about lawsuits. They had to have liability insurance. Prices went up, and we had to deal with moral, ethical, religious issues. We could no longer spend our time and love and energy on patients.

Then they began to fantasize—once the kidneys are really working, we'll transplant livers and then hearts and then brains and then we'll clone people. We can deep freeze our dying patients at the moment of death and keep them in the world. This was in the 1960s. They promised patients that 25 years from then, when there was a cure for cancer, we would defrost them and they would live happily ever after. This is not a fantasy novel; this actually happened. There are hundreds of people still in the vaults. In the 1960s it cost $9,000 a year to maintain them, and it has gone up to $40,000 a year. The whole process implied denial of death, a denial of mortality, and again that the rich could buy immortality and the poor had to die.

My minister friend and I philosophized over the problems we had at the university with lawsuits, and with physicians no longer being able to be physicians. In an impulsive moment, I said to him, "I'm going to spend the rest of my life working to find a definition of death. Because if we had a complete, absolute definition of death, we would have no more lawsuits."

Now, he was a minister, and I have always had problems with ministers. I told him, "You guys are always up in the pulpit, and you always say, 'Ask, and you will be given.' I'm asking now, how do you find a definition of death? How does a physician find an accurate, absolute definition, one without exceptions? For instance, a flat brain wave; but if you freeze to death, you can have a flat brain wave and then come back without damage." Within five days I got an answer, one that literally changed my life.

(Now I know that when your spiritual quadrant is open, if you ask you will receive. You will receive immediately, if you need it immediately, but you will not receive if you only want it. For example, once I was in San Francisco, and having talked nonstop for three days, I was hoarse. On my way to San Diego and the next morning to Europe, I was already thinking: I have one night, I'm going to unpack, do laundry, repack, take off. I did not want to hear any more. A woman came and pulled on my blouse and said, "Dr. Ross." All I wanted was to say, "My name is Mary Smith." I didn't say that, but she picked up on it immediately. She became desperate. She was with her young husband. She said, "We really, really need your help. In October our nine-year-old son died of cancer. He was our only son, and two weeks after his funeral our eleven-year-old was diagnosed to be full of cancer, beyond any treatment possibilities. All we can do is walk into her room and scream and yell at her and blame her for not even having given us permission and time and space to mourn our one and only son." They knew it was terribly wrong but they said they couldn't help it. What they said, really, was "We need help. Now."

I wanted to help this young couple so badly, but I knew if I didn't board the plane in the next five minutes, I would miss it, and I would miss the workshop in Europe. In utter despair, having more than I could handle, I said to myself (I would not even call it a prayer, at least not in those days), "God, if only I had one hour. Right here, right now." And in about 30 seconds, the loudspeaker came on and said, very matter-of-factly, "Flight 83 is delayed by one hour."

My whole life has been like this. My way to Austin to deliver this paper was utterly impossible to make. In Head Waters, Virginia, we were fogged in. In Stanton, we were fogged in. In Charlottesville, we were fogged in. I had to change hopper planes everywhere. Everywhere, there was thick fog; every plane was delayed. I arrived in Dallas 45 minutes late. My transfer time had been 50 minutes. In the Dallas airport you cannot make a connecting flight in 5 minutes when you have to go to another airline. I had come on Piedmont and I had to leave with American. I knew I was not going to make it. I thought of a thousand people sitting there, waiting, and me not showing up. I said, "Please, make a miracle happen, that I can make this connection. I absolutely need to be there." I didn't believe it, but it happens. I got off the plane, and the other airline, with my connecting flight, was right smack next door. I walked over and walked on the plane like it was nothing. Whether you're religious or not religious, there it is. What you call coincidences are not coincidences at all; you always get the help you need. If you don't need it, but only want it, then nothing happens. This is a marvelous differential diagnosis.)

The answer to my request for direction in my research on death came five days later. This was long before books were written and every magazine had stories about near-death and out-of-body experiences; I never knew those terms. A woman suffering a long- term illness who had been in the intensive care unit 15 times and never expected to live, came back to life again and shared with this minister and me the very first near-death experience I ever heard in my entire life. We were very excited; we knew this was an answer to prayer. Our fantasy was that if we could collect 20 cases like this, we could publish it in a journal of neurology or medicine, and it would change all of medicine. We were very naive in those days. We have collected 20,000 cases and still have not published the answer.

But I can share what all of you are going to experience at the moment of death. It does not matter where you come from or who you are, how much you have achieved, or whether you have been religious or not. This is a human experience, which is identical to the experience of birth in that all human beings are born basically the same way and have to go through the same tunnel to come to the light. Not symbolically but literally, with the exception of Caesarean sections.

In the memory of the children of Majdanek we use the image of the butterfly and the cocoon. How many of you are totally happy with the way you look? How many of you complain bitterly that you are too flat chested or your rear end is too fat or your legs are too thin or your hair is balding or your nose is crooked? That is not you. I don't know how many human beings there are on the planet earth, but the beauty of it is that everyone is different. Everybody is human, but still we are all a little bit different—that is one of creation's beauties. What makes us human is not the way we look. The real essence is inside and it's the only thing that counts.

Many, many children are afraid of being buried. They see on television that soil is put on the grave, and they think, "My God, Grandpa is going to suffocate," or they worry about themselves if they can conceive of their own deaths. We always tell them, and this is in memory of the children of Auschwitz and Buchenwald, that the only thing that is buried is your cocoon. The real you is going to leave at the moment of death. What happens when you die, and it does not matter how you die—whether it's a sudden death or a homicide or a suicide or a slow lingering death—is simply that the butterfly comes out of the cocoon.

I'm using symbolic language to share what happens at the moment of death. This is your physical life, requiring physical energy, and in order to function you need a functioning brain, and with a functioning brain comes consciousness. When your life is no longer viable, when your body is destroyed beyond any possibility of survival, whether due to a plane crash or a drowning or an avalanche or a coronary, what happens is that the cocoon releases the butterfly, the real you. That part is immortal and can never be destroyed. One's body may be in a thousand pieces, but at death you will immediately notice that you're totally whole.

Working with little children who have had leukemia, the first thing we hear if they've had a near-death experience is, "You know, I had my hair again." Children lose their hair when they have chemotherapy for leukemia, and this is the first thing they tell us. My multiple sclerosis patients who have been in wheelchairs for months and months say, "I was able to sing and dance again." So one becomes whole.

With physical life comes psychic energy, which can be a very dangerous, but also blessed energy. It all depends entirely on how it is used. Human beings have been given the greatest gift in life—free choice. What you do with that choice determines your life after death. We are one hundred percent responsible for our lives through the choices we make, not only in deeds but also in thoughts and in words. We can only manipulate physical and psychic energies. We cannot manipulate spiritual energy which is from God.

The near-death and out-of-body experiences like those described in the literature can only go so far, because beyond that the person does not come back and so we can't really know. At this stage, being out of body but not dead yet, one has no vital signs, but complete awareness. Someone in a coma who is on the verge of death, whose vital signs have ceased, is still totally aware—not only of what you are saying, but also what you're doing and what you're thinking. Awareness includes the knowledge of what people are thinking at the place where death has come. This is verifiable scientifically. One man, run over by a hit-and-run driver, saw his own amputated leg lying on the highway. But the real him had both legs and was whole again. He was the only case we have had so far of somebody who was able to give us the license number of a hit-and-run driver.

Things like this do happen. An accident victim can say, for example, how many blow torches were used to extricate them from a car so wrecked that rescuers cannot pull them out of the windows. We had a case in Switzerland of a man who was in a horrible car wreck and was declared dead at the scene of the accident. He overheard what people were thinking and discovered that they were mostly upset about being made late to a ball game. He was totally aware of their irritation at being delayed. Except, in the seventh car behind the accident, there was a woman who was totally absorbed in praying for him. She prayed that he would make it, and that he would get well. He almost cried as he described later how passionately this woman prayed for a total stranger. She didn't even know if it was a man or a woman, because they had covered him up. When he recovered he asked his doctor to help him find that woman. He found her and thanked her, and she was overcome to get such feedback, such evidence that prayers are heard and really help. We have many verifiable examples like this.

I am a skeptical scientist, but I say that you will be whole again. People who have had no light perception for ten years or more, who have not been able to distinguish even light and dark, can tell you what kind of a necklace or design of necktie you were wearing after they've had a near-death experience. They identify colors and describe the dresses and jewelry. This is not oxygen deprivation. That is the "rational" answer I get, and it is impossible.

A Native American woman was struck by a hit-and-run driver on a highway. She was lying on the side of the road, injured not visibly but internally. Hundreds of cars went by, and nobody stopped. Finally one man stopped, got out of his car, and asked, "Is there anything I can do for you?" She answered very calmly, "No, there is nothing else anybody can do for me." The beauty of it was that that he stayed with her; he did not leave her. He just stayed there. After a while she said, "Yes, there is something that one day maybe you can do for me. Visit my mother if you ever get near the Indian Reservation [which was 700 miles away] and tell her that I was okay." She used the past tense. Then after a while she said, "Tell her that I'm very happy because I'm already with my Dad." And then she died. This man was so moved at being in the right place at the right time that he drove 700 miles out of his way to the reservation. There, the mother of the victim told him that her husband had died just one hour before the car accident. When I heard this story, I got the message: my job was to find people who had near-death experiences, or who were near death and able to talk; I needed to find people who could not possibly have known that somebody in the family had died.

A very nasty 84-year-old lady was the most lovely lady before she had a near-death experience. When she came back she was an absolute monster. She gave everybody a terrible time, using vile language. She was very different from most people who come back after such a spiritual experience. Finally I was called in and was told "Something's happened to this woman. She's changed. We can't stand her anymore." I am very outspoken. I asked the old lady, "What happened to you when you went to the other side?" She said, "I'll tell you what happened to me. Those people didn't even have the guts to tell me that my beloved sister had died. I came back to give them hell." What had happened was that while she was in the hospital, her sister, who had lived with her for 70 years, had died. The hospital staff had decided not to tell the old lady, because they thought it would be too much for her. Then she had this near-death experience and her sister stood there; she was furious with them for not telling her and she came back just to give them a hard time!

So, for the past 13 years, after holidays, Labor Day weekends and such, when there are many family outings, I have done my research. A mother or a brother dies, an uncle or a grandma, at the scene of the accident, and other family members, especially children, are sent to intensive care units or burn units in very serious or critical condition. There, shortly before they die something happens to them. At the moment when I see this change I know they have peeked through to the other side. Then I ask, "Can you share with me what you experience?" They see right through me; they know why I ask that question. If they trust me, they say, "Everything is okay now. I have peeked at Mommy who is already waiting for me." And yet, they've not been informed who was killed at the scene of the accident. In 13 years I haven't had one single child mention somebody who did not precede him or her in death. If this were not reality it would be statistically impossible.

So I continue to share. Those who are ready to hear will hear it. The others will find out anyway when they die.

Everything here is real, but not reality. It's very important to know the difference. When you see people who died 20 years ago the way you had known them, then you understand that you don't exist in eternity in a physical body. They are recreated for you for the purpose of recognition, of knowing them again. That is a gift to you given with the same love parents have when they take the first grader to the schoolhouse before the first day of school so that the child will be familiar with it and not scared or nervous.

Once you have had your reunion, and once you know that death is not the end but the transformation into a different form of life, you create with your psychic energy the transition, something that is culturally determined, a gate or a bridge or a tunnel. Behind this tunnel is an incredible light. In a near-death experience, you can see a glimpse of that light, and it is absolutely and utterly impossible to be afraid of death. You can tell who has had the real experience, because if there is any fear of death left, then they are phonies, or they are making it up. Or they want to be interesting. Or they have read too many books.

You can go this far and still come back. In death, what happens is that the connection between the cocoon and the butterfly is severed. Then the cocoon closes, and in the presence of this light you are wrapped in total, absolute, unconditional love and a sense of total peace. There are no more desires. All you want is to stay there. This is a totally indescribable experience. But it's here that you have to review your life. This is where the quality of your life begins to make a difference. Because you have all knowledge, you will be totally and completely aware of every deed, every word you have ever spoken, and every thought you have ever had.

This is why children have to learn discipline early in life. If you have no discipline, and you do what you please, you will never learn to be aware of the effects of your thoughts. After you have mastered your negative behavior, and you've become a bit more civil and a bit nicer, you also have to watch your language. Then the last, and sometimes the most difficult lesson in life, is to be aware of how much you affect your environment with your thoughts. Our thoughts are very much alive. They're very real. If you're nasty early in the morning, and your kids don't get breakfast and you kick your husband out of the house without coffee, what happens? Your kids go out and kick the dog, and they're already angry on the way to school. Then they get into fights with the other kids, they irritate the teacher, the teacher sends them to the principal, and the principal sends them home with a letter. Your husband lets out his anger on his secretary who lets it out on her lover, and you know what it's like when they go home.

We deal with various major issues. Right now we are flooded with people who have AIDS. I am hoping to open a home for babies, AIDS babies. They are from six months to two-and-a-half years old, the offspring of drug-using mothers. The mothers are usually single, usually living a very marginal kind of life. They're not bad people but they just cannot handle a little child who needs 24-hour care, and who has AIDS. So they drop the child in a city hospital and then they leave without giving a forwarding address. And there are so very many babies. Far beyond what you can imagine.

Many people are not aware that we have two million carriers of AIDS in the United States already. Ten percent of these people will have AIDS within the next two years. The numbers are far bigger than any statistics can reveal, because most of them, about ninety percent of those I know, are not registered. They are parents who have had reasonable marriages and have a baby, and the baby is born with AIDS. Then the father is forced to confess that he was bisexual. This illness is so horrible a threat because it enters again into this field of honesty. It reveals one's whole private life. Nothing is hidden. Nothing is sacred anymore. Not Sacred sacred, but sacred sacred. It's very difficult to have an illness that is transmitted mainly, not exclusively, through intimate life. It stirs up all sorts of anxieties.

The children we want to take are the ones who are left in city hospitals. We get phone calls every day. I recently received a phone call from a very desperate woman who has a 17-month-old baby who has been rejected from 23 places in 17 months of life. What kind of a beginning is this? This child may live another year. And God! would I love to say, "Come to my place. I have home-cooked food, I have vegetables, I have sunshine, I have love. I have a room ready, full of toys and cribs, and we are sewing fancy colorful blankets." And I cannot take this child, because the whole community is ready to lynch me. I'm importing AIDS into this valley. The real-estate values will go down, tourism will decline, the water system will be flooded with the AIDS virus. They claim, "She's importing AIDS into the valley and she will destroy the whole valley." So they will do anything in the world not to have it there. Everybody says, "Why don't you have it in New York, why don't you have it in Austin, why don't you have it in San Diego, in California? Well, anywhere, but not here." And they refuse to give us the necessary rezoning.

My big human conflict is that I could very easily adopt 15 babies tomorrow. I could pick them up on my way home and take care of them, but that would be very negative. Our role has to be to get rid of fear and of guilt and shame and negativity, and we will not win if we use negative means to achieve our goal. So I have to learn patience. I know that all these children will be dead by the time I get the rezoning and the license, but it will serve a purpose for the townspeople to know that I'm not doing what I please, but am listening to their needs. That is perhaps the only way they will ever understand that there is no threat to them. That is the big conflict in our society today.

You get your basic attitudes between the ages of one and six. How many of you were allowed to grieve at this age? Grieving is a very healthy, natural gift with which to deal with losses early in life so that one will be prepared for bigger losses later in life. But what were you told when you cried when you were little? "It's a no-no." "Oh, that sissy, here she goes again and cries." "Oh, God, big boys don't cry." My favorite is, "If you don't stop crying, I'll give you something to cry about." I got that all the time, and it shuts one up immediately because you are petrified about what is coming if you don't stop. You end up marinating in self-pity, shame, guilt, and the "poor me" syndrome. But these depressions are preventable. If a child falls and is hurt and cries, you don't make a fuss. Take the three-year-old child who falls off a tricycle—she cries like somebody chopped off her head. If you don't make a big fuss she hops on the tricycle and drives off. But if you make a big fuss, or if you do the opposite—"Oh, poor girl," making a big deal out of it—she becomes a manipulator later on. The louder she cries, the bigger the toy. So neither extreme is healthy.

How many of us were allowed to be angry when we were little? What did you get? Spanking? What kind of torture tools did they use? Hands? You were lucky. Words, deprivation of love, ostracism, being sent to bed without dinner—these are also used. The torture tools include not only wooden cooking spoons, but belts with buckles, whips, and all sorts of things. I could assemble a collection of tools that are used on children which most people would not believe. There is so very much physical abuse in our country. Twenty-five percent of all grown-ups who come to my workshops have been sexually abused. This is an enormous number of people now grown up who have been physically and sexually abused, not to mention emotionally abused. How in the world can you be whole and feel good about yourself if you have been sexually abused? You try eventually to tell Mom, she hits you, and says, "Don't you ever talk about that, and don't you lie," and sends you to your room. You will never again dare to speak about it. Then 50 or 60 years later, sitting in a workshop, one woman dares to bring it up and release the burden and pain, and suddenly 15 people start sobbing and crying. And I thank that one person who had the courage to let go, because she gave a gift to all the others.

Little children are naturally jealous of the older brother who can play the accordian or sing better or write already. Pity turns into envy and jealousy, and envy and competition in love is the biggest problem of all. How many of you were raised with "I love you if . . . "? If. "I love you if. . . . " What were the ifs that you were raised with? If you behave? If you are seen and not heard? If you eat your spinach? If you clean up your room? If you bring good grades home? If you would finish high school? "I would really love you if I could say, 'My son, the doctor.' " So you become a doctor when you really wanted to be a carpenter or something else. I call that prostitution; prostitutes are those who do things to be loved.

I have seen thousands of people die, and a great, great majority of them say, "I made a good living but I've never really lived." I ask, "What do you mean, you never really lived?" They reply, with great sadness, "I became a very successful lawyer [or a very successful whatever], but I really wanted to do something else. But I never did it because my dad was so proud to be able to say, 'This is my son, the lawyer.' " They end up living their whole lives with the illusion that love can be bought. That is why I call it prostitution. One cannot buy love. No matter how sweet you are, how nicely you dress, how many titles you have, you will shop for love for the rest of your life. Those people are very, very sad because they always do things in expectation. Real love is unconditional, and that means no hooks, no claims, no expectations attached to it.

Something else that is very difficult for a lot of people is to say, "No." "No, I'm not tying your shoelaces until you're 13 years old. I have all the confidence in the world that you can do it." Children will manipulate, cry, will do anything, and this makes it very hard to parent consistently. Inconsistency is one day letting them get away with everything, and the next day, beating them up just for sneezing. What the child needs to grow up in a real way is unconditional love and firm, consistent discipline.

In the past, if a child came home with torn clothes, dirty shoes, and a runny nose, Mother stood in the door and said, "Just wait until Dad comes home" and you knew you were going to get it. But she didn't have the nerve to give it to you right away. You had to wait for hours until Father came home and spanked you. By then you didn't even remember what you were spanked for. But sometimes, during that waiting period, Grandma peeked her head out of the door and just looked at you, and you knew she loved you no matter if your clothes were torn, your shoes were dirty, and you had a runny nose. And sometimes she hugged you and all the yellow stuff went all over her face and she didn't care. Those are what we call moments, and it's almost always a grandma or grandpa, or an older generation person—it doesn't even have to be a relative. In present times, we don't have three-generation homes—at any rate, very few—because grandmas are in nursing homes or retirement centers, and we cheat children out of a unique source of unconditional love. When you are grandparents, it's much easier to love your grandchildren, because you don't have to live with them 24 hours a day and you are really not that directly responsible for them.

My dream is to have "ET" centers (ET means elderly–toddler) where single old people with no family can live free of charge in a loving, natural environment. The price they have to pay, not in cash but in love, is to care for one toddler. Skipping a generation eliminates so many problems. The grandma, the old person, has to love one child of her own choice—she picks which toddler to love—and she can spoil that child rotten but not with material things. They will not be allowed to buy toys. The elderly will pick the toddler up, take the little ones on their laps, and tell them about good old Texas or Ireland or Scotland or wherever they grew up. In exchange, the elderly get something very few old people get nowadays: they get talked to and touched again. Because children love wrinkles. They even like pimples. They play piano on them.

In exchange for this unconditional love, the old people are going to get love, and if they get love and hugs and touches, they do not become senile as fast as they do in our nursing homes. In nursing homes they are very often tied down on a chair, they are incontinent, and they feel useless. They don't really want to live but they also can't die. In the ET centers, they would have a purpose—they would be wanted, loved, needed. The gift that the mothers and fathers get is a place where they can take their child and then absolutely not worry, either about sexual abuse or that they have picked up a babysitter with some unknown pathology. If grandma gets a little stroke and can't function much anymore, the children are the first to say, "Where is Grandma?" They try everything to visit with grandma even if it's only for an hour. The availability of grandparents calms the parents who have to work, it gives the old people again somebody who really hugs and touches and loves them, and it gives the children the experience of unconditional love. This is the basic framework; if we can do this, then we will have fewer problems in this life and we will stay healthier much longer.

Naturally, parents do not expect their child to die. It's a horrible, horrible blow. They think if a child dies before reaching adolescence, it means that the child will never reach the intuitive inner knowledge. This is not so, because in life when you lose something, you always get something. Not on the same level, but you always, always get something when you lose something. Children who develop leukemia at age three and die at age nine have six years of terminal illness during which they develop very prematurely this intuitive spiritual power. They become very old, wise people. This is one of the beauties of human life. Although it is the body of a tiny little girl, their talk can sound like someone 70 years of age. Parents who share that reflection with other families are smiled at: "Oh, they're going to make a saint out of this child because he died." That is not true. These children are very wise people. They have an inner wisdom which probably exceeds that of most adults who have not suffered or been chronically ill.

Dying patients use three languages. First there is plain English. "I'm not going to be around at Christmas anymore." If you say to the dying person, "Oh, don't talk like this. You're going to get well," you immediately shut off the person who wants to share the knowledge of impending death. Many learning experiences are lost like this because dying people are marvelous teachers. Second, the dying may speak a symbolic language, verbal or nonverbal, when they realize that you cannot cope with plain English. An example of symbolic verbal language is a disguised message in the form of a parable. Jesus used parables because he knew that those who are ready to hear do hear. Those who are not ready still scratch their heads after 2,000 years.

Dying children think, "Maybe he's ready. I have to convey that I know I'm not going to get well, or that I'm not responding to this chemotherapy." Although intellectually they don't understand what cancer or chemotherapy is, internally they know. If they have a little bit of faith and hope that you are one who will not take off or play games, they will use the symbolic verbal language. If you really care, you will say, "I am not sure if I understand you. But is this what you're saying?" They will rephrase it until you understand. But if you know with your head and then talk about the weather, they know you are a phoney. It is as simple as that.

For example, when they cannot talk anymore, or if they trust a different way of communication, you can ask children to draw pictures. Jung discovered that spontaneous drawings reveal your whole inner knowledge of everything. There is an art to reading drawings; you can't just read them in half an hour. You have to train yourself, as more and more physicians are now doing. If you look at spontaneous poems by suicidal teenagers, you will see that probably every one of these children is trying to convey the suicidal intention to his or her parents. If you read it and don't understand, ask, and they will tell you what it is that you can do for them. It is not only parents who can help; somebody can.

Spontaneous poems, drawings, and collages are the language of dying children, dying teenagers, suicidal teenagers, and the siblings of murdered children. People in great pain cannot talk about it because it's simply too painful. So they use this language, and if we can begin at least to know that it exists, we will be able to help many, many children. Suicide, in this most blessed country of the world, is the third cause of death for children between 6 and 16 years of age; many, not all, of these are preventable.

Now I am spending about half of my time working with dying children all over the world, and with parents of murdered children, who do not get any help because nobody knows what to say to them. I work with parents whose children have committed suicide. I listen to their guilt, their regrets, their "if I had onlys. . . . " It's absolutely incredible. I always say fear and guilt are the biggest enemies of man. We really need to get rid of them.

If we want to create a new society, we need to grow a generation of children who are not afraid of living or of dying. If we could do that, it would all be very simple. And the only way to bring peace into the world is by starting inside ourselves. Not outside. Let us practice loving each other.

CHAPTER THREE

My Mother and My Father

Mary Catherine Bateson

Adapted from a lecture and discussion entitled "With a Daughter's Eye: A Memoir of Margaret Mead and Gregory Bateson" at the Institute for the Humanities at Salado, September 29, 1985.

About Mary Catherine Bateson

Mary Catherine Bateson's paternal grandfather, William Bateson, was a pioneer geneticist, who coined the name of the new science and set up a center for genetic research in London. Her father, Gregory Bateson, was an eminent cultural anthropologist. And her mother, Margaret Mead, was an even more famous anthropologist, whose writings are widely known.

On September 29, 1985, Bateson spoke at the Salado Institute about the challenge of writing *With a Daughter's Eye: A Memoir of Margaret Mead and Gregory Bateson.* Describing her extraordinary childhood growing up under the influence of her famous, very different, highly intellectual and terribly busy parents, she examined their effect upon her as role models and upon her own attitude in rearing her daughter.

In her informal lecture and in answers here incorporated to questions from the audience, Bateson touched on the controversy over some of Margaret Mead's research and conclusions; human genetics; the extended family; the masculine/feminine spirit and sex roles in our society and in other societies; lifelong parenting; and the importance of conversation between parents and children in creating rather than implanting knowledge and in stimulating the ability to think.

Dr. Bateson, then professor of anthropology at Amherst, received her undergraduate degree from Radcliffe in 1960 and a Ph.D. from Harvard in 1963. She has conducted research at Brandeis and M.I.T., taught at Harvard and Northeastern, and been involved in educational planning for various institutions in Iran. Her publications deal with linguistics and anthropology. Her books are *Structural Continuity in Poetry: A Linguistic Study of Five Pre-Islamic Odes,* (Hague: Mouton, 1970); *Our Own Metaphor: A Personal Account of a Conference on the Effects of*

Conscious Purpose on Human Adaptation (New York: Knopf, 1972); *With a Daughter's Eye: A Memoir of Margaret Mead and Gregory Bateson* (New York: William Morrow and Co., Inc., 1984; Pocket Books, 1985) and *Angels Fear: Towards an Epistemology of the Sacred* (New York: Macmillan, 1987; Bantam Paperbacks, 1988); *Thinking AIDS* (with Richard Goldsby) (New York: Addison-Wesley, 1988, paperback, 1989).

   Dr. Bateson's current position is at George Mason University where she is the Clarence Robinson Professor in Anthropology and English. She is also president of the Institute for Intercultural Studies in New York.

   My book has been out for a bit more than a year. I've just made the decision to take a year or so off from teaching to do some more writing. I've just been arranging that, and thinking through what I want to do next. I am going to share with you a writer's between-book reflections, about how one gets from one book to the next. After all, writing the memoir *With a Daughter's Eye* about my mother and my father is not a trick I can repeat. I'm never going to have material of that kind of immediacy and interest again. I have written other books, and there are other things I know I want to do. In a sense I blundered rather naively into this book with no real reflection on the amount of introspection it would require or the number of complicated and painful memories that I would have to work through. It was a very intimate, personal task.

   I was in Iran when they had their revolution. I returned to the United States, a whole period of my career brought to an end. My mother had just died. My father had already had a major brush with death from cancer now apparently in remission, but he was living on borrowed time. And there I was, wondering, "What am I going to try to do next?" At that time there were signs of a new industry developing: turning out biographies of Margaret Mead. There have, in fact, been three, in a sense four, since her death, not counting mine, which is not a biography. I was not prepared for a full-time career of being interviewed by biographers, but I could not simply say no. So I said, "I can't talk to you because I am going to write my own book." Then I thought, "Well, I will write this, but I will write it about both parents, not about my mother who was the more famous." I made that decision with relatively little reflection about what it would mean to undertake such a task after the death of one's parents. I also made that decision with very little reflection about the topic I wish to discuss here, the difference between focusing on one parent and focusing on two.

I would like to continue the kind of writing I think I did in this book: combining discussion of the content of people's work with discussion of personal relationships, and doing so comparatively.

We live in a period when biography is a major industry. Actually, gossip is a major industry. This is true from the intellectual slums right up to the ivory towers. People are writing biographies. One need only look at the literary supplement of Sunday *New York Times* or other major book reviews to realize how much work is being done in the field of biography. Furthermore, many biographies of women are being written, at a time when all across the United States women are dealing with changes in roles, possibilities, and aspirations and lack proximate models. Many women choosing careers, either young women coming out of school or going back to school after their children are grown, have few helpful models. Their mothers did not necessarily help them think out how to be a professor, a businesswoman, a politician, or whatever they are going to be. There may have been very few such women models nearby. So people want to read biographies of successful women, mainly focusing on the last century. Reading biography is a way of taking someone to yourself. Then they are available as a part of the mosaic from which you construct your own identity.

I was staying with friends in Dallas recently, and my host said to me, "I've always been interested in biographies of intellectuals, life histories of intellectuals, and I've added your book to my collection." I asked, "Why? Why is that something that you like to read?" He answered immediately and glibly, "They are guides to right action." Now most of us think this way: when we talk about role models, we think of emulating others, following in people's footsteps. I find this very problematic. I raised my eyebrows. He has about a hundred biographies on the shelf where he collects them. I asked him if he needed that many guides to right action. He thought about it for a minute, then said, "You know, that's not really true. It is not that they are guides to right action. They are countries I like to visit. They are ways of entering another experience and spending time there." That is certainly part of the issue.

But it does seem to me that we are rather seriously afflicted with the idea that people grow up with single models. Maybe this is a legacy of the years of increasing dependency on isolated nuclear families. Often a person will speak of someone who was "my idol," "my hero," when growing up. It could be a parent or, in my generation, Babe Ruth or John Kennedy or Eleanor Roosevelt; often it is just one inspiring figure.

I had a very peculiar experience from that point of view. We all know something about the problems people have in dealing with a famous parent. A famous parent is a complicated thing to have in one's life. But what about two? Furthermore, what about two who, as in the case of my parents, passed through a period of conflict, separated from each other, and were for all their similarities profoundly different in intellectual and personal style? This is a very different problem, a very different challenge, but on the whole I think it is a huge help. I recommend to anyone affiliated with one famous parent that they acquire a second one.

I have often wondered what it would have been like to be the son of my mother (she had no sons), without a father present. My father had two other children, both of whom found being his child far more complicated than I did, because he was the giant figure on the scene. In a way, the fact that I was trying to make sense out of the two of them was my salvation. Sons of famous fathers often feel that they must compete with their fathers. In this culture, with its emphasis on competition and achievement for young males, this is more of a problem for sons of famous fathers than for daughters of famous mothers. Because what is implicit in our culture is that, of course, since your mother was so extraordinary, it being so unusual for a woman to achieve that much, you really don't have to compete; her achievement is not likely to happen again. This is not what young males experience. They feel that at some level they have to try and outdo their towering fathers. That's very problematic.

In any case, we know that women of high achievement tend to feel that emulating their fathers is what has been important to them. But otherwise there is a traditional notion that we emulate our same-sex parent. We have very intense relationships with the parent of the opposite sex, complicated in all sorts of ways. But we learn social roles from the parent of the same sex. Again, there occurs the same notion of one principle model.

Recently I had a conversation with a friend who is a geneticist. We talked about the puzzle of bisexual reproduction, which is really a very peculiar way of doing things. Whenever things work out successfully and there is a good genome, a good working formula, what happens? You reshuffle the cards. The pair of individuals manages to reproduce; they're surviving; they're doing well. But their offspring will not be quite the same. We talk about DNA as self-replicating, but the genome of individuals is not based on simple self-replication. It's a new combination that doesn't match either of the parents. You might well think, "That's an awful mistake! Just a very bad way for the living world to be organized. You should find the right answers, institutionalize them, and clone them! In large numbers! Get rid of the shuffling!"

We laughed, but in fact we shift all too often into thinking, "You work out the right way to do it, and then you repeat it." But that doesn't seem to be how the natural world does it. There is a kind of reshuffling that happens. I have always been fascinated by the fact that there are so many myths that connect the origin of death to sexuality, in one form or another, because in fact these two are logically connected. Bisexual reproduction with its reshuffling of the genes does eventually require getting rid of the previous batch. The only alternative is keeping the successful products around indefinitely, in which case one would not want to produce new ones.

I relate this rather striking fact to the question of whether it is really a good thing to have a hero, a model. I'm not sure that it is. This business of heroes has been puzzling me since the Kennedy assassination. Kennedy was killed, and in the circles in which I moved, people went into deep mourning, all convinced that he had been absolutely wonderful. But I knew what those same people had been saying two weeks before. They were full of criticism. They might have voted for him, they might have been pro-Kennedy, but only after his death did they find it necessary to endow him with heroic qualities. I was inclined to say, "Yeah, he was pretty good and I'm sorry he was killed and he stood for some important things, but I remember what I felt last week." That was an unpopular attitude.

It should not have surprised me, a few years later, that there were massive attacks on Kennedy. A great deal of demythologizing took place. There was a first round of turning him into a hero, and a second round of discovering that strong as he was in some ways, he was not perfect, and that the hero-worship was inappropriate and also exaggerated. This is a process we go through again and again. It is a process that has been very striking to me particularly in relation to my mother, but to some extent in relation to my father. He was far less widely known, but showed every sign of becoming a cult figure in California.

I keep saying, "Yes, I loved them. They were terrific. I learned a lot from them. But you're not saying they were perfect, are you?" There were those people who felt that the tower in the American Museum of Natural History in New York, where my mother was officed, should be kept intact as she left it. (She was very clever about dealing with competitive male colleagues; she picked her bit of territory so far off the beaten path nobody wanted it. She held onto her tower office for almost 50 years and gradually expanded it—into the corridors.) Some people felt vehemently that such was her stature, as the most important scholar who had ever been associated with the American Museum of Natural History, that the museum should keep her office untouched, in the state in which she left it, as a shrine. After all, she had put American anthropology on the map.

I found myself saying, "Look, do you know what real estate is worth in New York City? Do you know what every square foot in that museum represents in terms of the needs of the public, like that of school-children, to visit the museum?" When I was a kid, it was an empty museum, and I had it almost to myself. Now there's not a hall that isn't jammed with people. There has been a terrific increase in demand on the same space and the same real estate the museum had before. The nerve of anyone who thinks some of that space should be turned into a shrine! Especially since, in order to get to that shrine, people would have to go through two long corridors that are closed to the general public, and there would have to be a whole new system of guards, tours, and so forth. I found myself at odds with some really splendid people whose deter-mination was to create a memorial. I had to say, "Well, that's a very nice idea, but it isn't something she would have liked." She would have said to let the museum use the space. She was not the kind of person who would have wanted to be enshrined.

It also makes me a little nervous when people associated with the California Zen community want to build shrines to my father. I keep saying, "No, and no, and no." And they look at me as if I were perhaps lacking in filial piety, or even worse, spiritual insight.

I think there is a relationship between the fact that I grew up with many available models, of whom the two most important were my parents, and the fact that I don't feel such a need to construct heroes. A few years before my book came out, an Australian anthropologist named Derek Freeman brought out a book that was a violent attack upon my mother's work on Samoa. Now, I don't know anything about Derek Freeman's relationship to his mother, but I do know that he had a problem with my mother for years. He did anthropological work in Samoa; when people asked, "Where do you do your research?" he would say, "Samoa," and they would respond, "Oh, yes, I've read Margaret Mead. Isn't she wonderful?" He shook and shivered and conducted guerrilla attacks over a period of about 40 years. Then after her death he launched a major attack.

It never occurred to me, when the book came out, that it would be gleefully seized upon by the very same people who had written embarrassingly adulatory obituaries when my mother died. In other words, Freeman's book became the center of a backlash of reaction. The reason this did not occur to me was that my feeling was, "Why yes, of course she made mistakes in her work in Samoa. She was only 23, and she was inventing a new field technique. That was 50 years ago. If we can't do better than that now, we're in trouble. So isn't it wonderful that somebody else is doing some work on Samoa and some of the errors will be corrected, the omissions will be rectified, and our scientific record will be more complete?"

That was a very naive response. Generally speaking, people want to attack or defend. They either wanted to dismiss the whole record and say Margaret Mead has been debunked, finished; or to defend the record in its entirety. It took quite a while (and there was a lot of shuffling around in the professional community that never made the national press) to work out a shared understanding that yes, of course, there were flaws in the Samoan work, but nevertheless it was pioneering work and my mother's stature as a scientist could survive that criticism. Derek Freeman's criticisms were based on some very shoddy scholarship. Maybe the corrections could be better done by someone who was not driven by an obsession that had to do with something in his own childhood—and the feeling that it was much, much more fun to trash Margaret Mead than to do careful scientific work and write a monograph about Samoa, which he has yet to do.

When my mother was in Samoa she studied mainly adolescents. She was interested in the question of whether adolescence is necessarily in all cultures a period of strong upheaval, of conflict and violence and stress, or whether a large component of this is culturally produced. On the whole, her position affirmed the nonuniversality of certain kinds of adolescent behavior. The position of people like Freeman is that the stress of adolescence is entirely biologically produced, having everything to do with hormonal, that is, biological changes in the body and nothing to do with cultural influences. It is certainly the case that the increase in certain kinds of stress during adolescence, although it can be greater or less in a given culture, is recurrent. But Margaret Mead insisted on the malleability of human behavior.

One thing neither Mead nor Freeman ever thought of: almost all of the literature on adolescence available at the time of my mother's work was based on all-male research populations. In other words, all those books about adolescence have turned out to be books about *male* adolescence. Quite often in psychology the sampling procedure is simplified by limiting it to males.

Margaret Mead looked at a sample and generalized from it, just as others had, but her sample consisted of female adolescents. In other words, she made the mirror-image mistake. What is principally wrong with her picture of Samoa is that not knowing, as we now do, how different groups within even a preliterate culture can have different attitudes and emphasize different themes, she looked at a single group and extrapolated it to the whole society. Anthropologists have always done that: they talk to the chiefs and other important men and then describe the tribe, having talked only to the chiefs. She made the same mistake, with a less fashionable population. The chiefs may be pretty naive about their daughters.

In any case, she was interested in the fact that, as she saw it, these young Samoan women did not find adolescence a very stressful time; she felt that one of the reasons was that the sexual environment was very permissive compared to that of this country, where there was a great deal of repressive morality at that time. Samoa was also permissive in a different sense than, for example, we are now, because girls weren't under nearly the same pressure to start sexual activity that they are here. Even after the sexual revolution, attitudes toward sexuality during adolescence in this country are still stressful and demanding though perhaps in an opposite direction. The idea that you could move along at your own pace in a relaxed sort of way tends to escape us. A young Samoan girl would say, "I am but a child. Don't bother me." If only our daughters in junior high school, and our sons as well, could say that a little more often.

Mead saw the Samoan attitude toward sexuality as a factor affecting sexuality there. Another factor she discussed was the unchanging nature of Samoan society. There had not been a great deal of Western influence, so people grew up knowing what their lives were going to be like. They did not feel they had to make decisions, or try desperately to get into a particular school, or into whatever program people saw as the key to success. Life just fell into place, another factor which reduced stress during adolescence.

A third factor was that Samoan youngsters grew up in extended families that were very open to people who weren't part of the household. These families included neighbors, relatives, and other members of the community. There was a lot of coming and going, and if by any chance there was conflict in the household, one could move in with someone else. Even in this country, some adolescents do that. When relationships with mother and father become unbearable, they spend a year with an uncle or an aunt, which often proves to be salvation for the whole family. It is not a bad idea, for the nuclear family produces very intense hothouse relationships. In Samoa, routine permission to move in and out was a major way of reducing tension.

Now if the truth be told, my mother found those young Samoan girls a little bit too relaxed, too laid back, and even sometimes a little bit dull. She liked tensions in moderate degree and ambition. But she set up the household in which I grew up in such a way that I had perhaps five primary parents and another dozen significant peripheral parents, people who sustained long-term, loving responsibility for me. I spent months at a time in their houses or maybe two or three days a week over a period of years. My book, *With a Daughter's Eye,* about my two biological parents, is dedicated to my godmother, who was my mother's best friend in college, because her household really was my second home. During the war we lived in the household of Lawrence Frank, and his wife Mary Frank brought me up with their younger son Colin. In fact, I got six siblings out of that one. There were a whole series of other households that were home to me. Now, I will not deny that the really intense relationships that are central for me to understand have been the ones with my parents. All of the other relationships were less loaded, regardless of time spent. But still and all, there were many relationship models available to me, any one of which could supply something missing or defuse conflict in another relationship. There is a direct connection between family organization and the need for heroes who then have to be demythologized.

I am inclined to think that this presence of multiple models, quite aside from my parents being famous, was very important to me. It is something I hope we will work toward as a civilization, sort of building on the fact that, as nature does, it is good to shuffle the cards. No one wants to be exactly like any one admired person; one must combine a bit from here and a bit from there, and become something new.

A kind of pluralism of persons to emulate makes a great deal of biological and social sense. It has a vast advantage because on the whole most parents are pretty inadequate as models, and yet relationships to parents are often so close that one cannot afford to be critical. Unacknowledged ambivalence becomes problematic. Most parents, and I would include myself, deserve love, but so do they deserve ambivalence. Close relationships are like that.

I blundered into the notion that it was possible to write a book about my parents that would be both loving and critical. They were divorced, so I had to know that something was wrong somewhere. In fact, there was a great deal to be critical about. My father was married twice after he and my mother divorced, and there was a good deal of interpersonal messiness and stress over the years. Even as my mother had significant and important relationships with men, she had important intimate relationships with women and a pattern of sustained bisexuality. It was not that society required one thing and Margaret wanted the other. It was not a compromise. It was a pattern that she kept replicating.

My father was a very problematic person to love, because he was so self-absorbed. If I was interested in what he was interested in, he would spend infinite amounts of time with me. But when I tried to get him interested in what I was interested in, I lost him. I would go away, and I believe months went by when it never occurred to him to wonder what I was doing or where I was, in what country. Then I'd be with him and he would be absolutely superb and loving.

Margaret was really very busy with her public career, being elected president of associations and dashing off around the world being a public figure. She, too, was marvelously available in a few dimensions, but she was away an awful lot. It wouldn't have been very satisfactory, I think, to have been totally dependent on either one of them or to attempt absolute admiration of either of them. Although they were tremendously creative, they were very difficult people.

I think it was a miracle that my parents' marriage lasted as long as it did. They met in New Guinea on the Sepik River, when Margaret was still married to her previous husband. The initial courtship took place there. Then Gregory went to England and she went off to the United States. Eventually they arranged to meet for a vacation in Ireland together. She packed a beautiful trousseau to go to New Guinea that included silk underwear trimmed with lace. Gregory used that to wrap his lenses in. Did he ever give her a diamond? No. She had a ring that I think might have been a present from him, because I believe it came from Bali. It was a star sapphire she wore for years and years. In fact, I said to her once, "Without that ring you wouldn't be my mummy."

They split up right after World War II. They never really reunited after the war although they did live together for about a year. I think at that point the problem was that Gregory was not motivated, not goal-oriented. He had an unhappy war. Margaret had a wonderful time. Many people did enjoy the war; it was a time when they could use their talents in all-out efforts; women worked in factories, and everyone used everything they had to share in this very exciting work. She had a role in which everything she did was positive. He was in Southeast Asia in psychological warfare. That is, instead of using his anthropological training to further communications among the Allies and sustain civilian morale as she did, using knowledge constructively, he was using knowledge to further disinformation, creating confusion and fear in the enemy. They were both very concerned about winning the war. But he came out of the war quite depressed and without a sense of what his goals were. He was very much at loose ends and she was not.

Their energy levels were also very different. She was extremely energetic, while he was a low-energy person. Most of the time he didn't know what he was doing, or where his thinking was going. He played with ideas in the back of his mind. Eventually they came out in an exciting way.

She, on the other hand, would see a social problem and say, "We'll organize, we'll get some new ideas, and we'll solve it." He would say, "When you try to solve problems usually you make them worse."

They were complementary; the contrast was very great, but up to a certain point it was helpful to both of them. She always thought he was much smarter than she was, but she had the energy, the attention to detail, and the capacity to work with institutions. He had the deeper intellect. This view I think they actually both shared.

I was 10 or 11 years old when my parents divorced. At that point my father had been living in California for two years, but he had moved out of the house when I was eight. The break happened in installments. People are much more efficient about these things nowadays. I had to work through feelings of resentment; when I wrote the book, the temptation was to view it all as lovely, but there were difficult and painful periods. On balance I think I came out ahead, and the benefits of my unusual situation outweighed the deficits. But what child does not hurt for the deficits regardless of the benefits?

I think the salvation for me was my mother's desire to replicate that Samoan network of extended family. In our case it was with elective ties of friendship rather than kin ties, and it was not unrelated to her desire to be free to pursue her career. It was a very sensible way to do this. But she quite specifically thought that it was a bad thing for children to be locked into the emulation and close relationships of the nuclear family.

If one grows up in an unusual environment, it may take quite a while to figure out how very unusual it is. It wasn't until my book came out and I read some of the comments of reviewers that I fully realized how strange my experience seemed to others. Much of my experiences I took for granted.

For example, my mother kept notes on my development. She was interested in child development, and she did some things which weren't done routinely because she had looked at child care in many other cultures. She kept very careful notes. The reviewer from *Newsweek* was absolutely horrified. Instead of the nice, warm, fuzzy-minded mother he remembered, the reporter envisioned somebody observing me with steely eyes and writing down every detail. As if there were an intrinsic conflict between tenderness and intelligence! We would be rather badly off if there were. It had never occurred to me that her note-taking would be horrifying to people. I took some rather good notes on my own daughter's linguistic development. They led to some good publications. My grandmother never published her notes on my mother's development, but she did write them down. The process seemed rather ordinary to me.

I was the first breast-fed, self-demand baby Ben Spock saw. The return to breast-feeding was just beginning when I was born in 1939. I am grateful to have been a breast-fed, self-demand baby; by the time I breast-fed my daughter it was the routine for educated mothers, but in those days it was rather unusual.

The way my parents brought me up influenced the way I have raised my own daughter in many ways. My husband and I moved around to different countries. That was hard. I believed my daughter could accept surrogates, and I arranged for them and tried to set up multiple important relationships for her with other people. But I have not left her for extended periods as my mother did me in my childhood. I like to think of the other relationships as additions. I did not want to burden her as I was burdened with people disappearing for six months at a time when I was two years old.

What I was most impassioned about wanting to preserve, and to make clear in my book, were the ways in which each of them taught me different kinds of things. My father taught me to look at natural history, to go to the woods, build an aquarium, and also taught me to think logically about categories and philosophical issues. My mother taught me to look at human differences and enjoy them, which I suppose is why I am in anthropology today. I cannot stop looking.

In my book I discuss my efforts to construct something that was equivalent to what she did. But the situation was different, so I had to work out an equivalent. The overarching issue was, how do you teach a child to be tolerant of differences in customs? I had to do that when I took my daughter with me at age two to live with a working-class Iranian family in a village. My mother never took me with her to the field. It was in New York that she taught me to be tolerant of human differences. But I see it as the same task. And I see it as immensely important and interesting not only to have warm, trusting relationships between parent and child, but to have this kind of learning going on all the time. I think one of the things that people find peculiar in my book is that there is so much talk about ideas.

It was terrific to grow up in an environment of intense talk. Those who think I talk a lot may not think it was so wonderful. One of the critical things for me was seeing my parents arguing with each other. Where I grew up, "argue" was a good word. I came home and said, "I had a huge argument with so-and-so and it was really exciting!" It didn't mean conflict; it meant that there were different views and I struggled with them. I watched my parents argue in that sense, grappling with something problematic. I watched them seek new understanding. That's what thinking is.

Gregory wrote a series of dialogues between a father and daughter. They deal with very abstract issues in communication and logic. The little girl, who is largely but not entirely fictional, keeps asking very naive questions that are very important in arriving at answers. Who would be so dumb as to be surprised at the idea of an apple falling from a tree? It takes genius to be surprised at such things.

So I think what was critical was the sense of conversation not as an implanting of knowledge but as the creation of knowledge, the moving to new knowledge. Both Gregory and Margaret made it clear to me in different ways that they expected to learn from conversations with me. They let me know that the questions I asked would force them into new paths of thought. My mother used to interview me when she wanted to understand what was happening among American children: "Now, Cathy, I understand there have been some problems at your school about this and that. Sit down and I'm going to interview you." I knew something she didn't know.

I think almost everything we say about school is based on the fallacy that you go to school to learn specific things, when in fact you should ideally be learning to think. What is critical is learning to learn, not learning particular facts.

Neither of my parents was ever interested in any kind of sport or exercise. My mother's approach to life was simple: "Never stand if you can sit; never sit if you can lie down. Save your energy for your mind." Gregory did long-distance running in school, which allowed him to go into the woods. The minute he got out of the master's sight he started to collect butterflies and beetles. Neither of my parents had reasonable physical skills.

Instilling in children an awareness of their own bodies is something we are currently doing well. I would not want anybody to think I advocate that they simply talk and talk and talk to their kids. Conversation is not a substitute for other kinds of learning.

One of the deficiencies of my childhood was in learning to move. When I was a child, girls were not as involved in sports. I grew up knowing almost nothing about any sport. At some point I figured out that people seemed to care about baseball, so I looked it up in the encyclopedia. I did not know how to ride a bicycle. I did not know how to drive a car until I graduated from college. Most American kids seem to take machines for granted. What one has and what one does not have is a very complicated mix.

In my social, emotional, and cultural development the "other people" were very important. There was much my parents and I both knew I was not going to learn from them. When I started getting interested in using makeup I checked with my mother to see if she minded. She said, "I don't think I can teach you how to do that. Why don't you go talk to your Aunt Pam?" Pam was Margaret's younger sister who was voted "Most Beautiful Girl" at the University of Wisconsin. Mother believed in finding the person who could best teach you the particular thing you wanted to know. She didn't teach me to sew or cook. Aunt Marie taught me those things.

Personality development as a whole is more complicated to discuss than specific skills. I grew up in an environment where I not only had to deal with a very wide range of people, but also for better or worse I had to please them. After all, most of them were not obligated to care about me. Margaret used to say, "The other mothers ask if they can borrow you because their children play so happily when you are there." It has long been said that children in orphanages bestow gorgeous smiles upon visitors. One learns to adapt.

Another dimension of this has to do specifically with sex roles. I had a hard time. I actually thought that most sensible people thought males and females were equal, and that right-thinking people would always do their best to make sure there were equal opportunities for males and females to develop their talents and use them. Now I know that this isn't true. It was, I think, splendid to grow up not thinking of myself as handicapped, and yet it was a handicap to be so unrealistic about how the world really works.

But clearly neither of my parents fit, in a simple sense, ideals of maleness and femaleness in our society. Remember, I was born in 1939. I was a teenager "going steady" in the 1950s. Much that we take for granted today was not yet widespread. Margaret and Gregory didn't fit. At the same time that they were so impressive and admirable, each of them in different ways was busy breaking the mold of standard expectations about what a man or woman is like.

Now there are many households in which the parents are determined that the boys should not be raised to be male chauvinists, and the girls should not be taught to be docile and pleasing and accept inferiority. There are many households in which couples have discussed how to make the division of labor in the family fairer. They both leave and go off with briefcases in the morning, and they both fix casseroles on alternate nights. Then they wash the dishes together.

Some people are worried and ask, "What's going to happen to the children? How are the children going to find out that men and women are different? They're confused about gender roles." This seems to me a splendid idea. There is one thing we can count on: even though both of those people make casseroles, they will specialize in different casseroles. Even though they both leave in the morning with briefcases, chances are their careers will have different shapes. It is simply impossible that any given family that works out a formula for sharing tasks will work out a formula of identical roles. One thing we can say about parents—they are different. Most relationships develop complementary dimensions as well as symmetrical dimensions. One of the things I think will happen is that young males growing up in this society will look increasingly at both parents as models to be emulated. I think young females will look at both parents as models to be emulated. Increasingly they will have permission to construct their identities from what they can draw from both parent figures, gender and sexual orientation being only one component of the total outcome. Genomes are restructured by shuffling the cards. My daughter Vanni had a job as a mechanic for a while, and I really hoped she would stay with it long enough to become a good one.

I feel that even children in two-parent households need to have other parent figures also. I didn't have my daughter until I was 30 years old. At that time, thirty was a bit late, although it is very common now. Before our daughter was born I realized that there weren't any small children in my life, and that I did not know how to talk to them. We had put off having children and I began to worry about it. What, I wondered, will happen when I have one? I was afraid I would be incapable of adjusting to a baby when we got around to it.

So I looked around and said, "Now who do I know that needs an aunt?" I found three or four children of friends, children from large families who did not have much chance to be alone with their parents, who I thought might like to be invited out singly for an afternoon or an overnight at my house. There are many adults who need children in their lives, elderly people and those who are deferring having children. And there are children who need additional adults, as do those growing up in single-parent households.

When families are blended, sometimes people are territorial about the influence of other people on their children. It is a problem. Margaret used to say that when she left me with Mary and Larry Frank during the war years, people said to her, "But Margaret, how can you dare to leave your child with a younger and more beautiful woman?" They assumed the natural response to that was jealousy; this is cultural. She said she was not inclined to jealousy.

We have trained people to be as possessive about children as they are about their shoes: not to want the imprint of somebody else's foot in their shoes, not to want the imprint of other people's parenting on their children.

So we hire menials, preferably from the least privileged of social groups, as surrogates. We do not treat them as colleagues in caring for our children any more than we welcome additional parenting from an ex-husband's new wife. We also hire teenagers, which is another way of employing persons we do not have to treat as equals. Women are willing to hire menials to fill in for them rather than allow the caretaker to be a full participant in their child's development. Unless we can get beyond this kind of possessiveness, we will not in fact be able to allow pluralism of models. My mother used to say that American women treat their refrigerators as if they were their own bodies: they cannot stand anyone else putting things in there. How can two women collaborate in the same household when they have this hang-up about the refrigerator?

It is hard on a child to be put with a babysitter, and when he or she shows off something learned, to be told "Our kind of people don't do that." It is amazing that English children can be taught so effectively not to emulate the speech of their nannies and the other servants who look after them. It is a very tricky business, a double bind, to put a child at risk of rejection for learning from a role model.

Many parents reject their adolescents' experimentation with alternate sexual orientations. But with pluralistic learning one's children will be different from oneself in some ways.

Traditionally, in the United States, children were sent to school because the teachers knew more than the parents did. Parents were often immigrants and the schoolteacher might be the most educated person in town. This opened doors. The schoolteacher was not totally supportive, unconditionally loving; indeed, love from a schoolteacher was precisely conditional. Today the difference between the role of the teacher and the parent has eroded. We are far more concerned than we were a generation ago with whether or not teachers are loving, and maybe insufficiently concerned with whether or not they are challenging our children to grow and learn. I do not know what the long-term effects of this blurring of the roles of teacher and parent will be.

I do not think there is a certain point at which parenting should end. We are relatively unique among civilizations in our insistence on pushing our children out of the nest. I believe parent–child relationships may be allowed to continue. Then there is the parenting of one's parents and the parenting of oneself. I do not think that parenting should ever end.

In this country we tend to see accepting ourselves as adults and continuing to rely on our parents for approval, leadership, or guidance as contradictory. I don't see these things as contradictory in a simple way. When I was 16 years old I went to live in Israel and did not see either parent for a year. I learned Hebrew and graduated from an Israeli school, and after that I never felt that I had to prove I could do without them. I just went away, and then we could be friends. I got all sorts of support from them because I had flown the coop. That is one way of doing it, and on the whole, it was very nice to have resolved the complicated issue of independence and leaving home at 16.

I remember when I came back from Israel after the year's absence, having been through a war. I was staying in my mother's house in New York, I had gone out on a date, and I came in at 2 A.M. to find my mother sitting up, stewing. "What's happened? Why are you out so late?" I looked at her and said, "You must be crazy." She replied, "You know, you are right. But whenever you are staying in this house if you're out late I am going to worry about you. That's the way it is. So please tell me when you're going to be late, okay?" I think there is a kind of balance in that.

Once when I was in high school, I went to visit my father in California and he was running a seminar in his living room for psychiatric residents at Stanford. At some stage I got passionately involved in an argument and moved in on the discussion, somewhat to people's surprise. At the end of the evening one of those residents looked at me and said, "My God, I always wondered what would happen if a lion and a giraffe mated." The thing that I have wondered long and often is what would have happened if I had had to deal with only one of those two people as a model.

Excerpts from *With a Daughter's Eye: A Memoir of Margaret Mead and Gregory Bateson*

It seems to me in retrospect that Margaret's willingness to make innovations came out of a certainty of her own love, a sense that she had been loved and could trust herself to love in turn, with a continuity of spontaneous feeling even where she was introducing variation. She was prepared to take responsibility because she did not suspect herself of buried ambivalence either toward me or toward her own parents. Indeed, in a life lived in an era of introspection and self-doubt, her conviction of undivided motives was distinctive, an innocence that leaves me sometimes skeptical and sometimes awed. Just as all of her commentaries about American culture and suggestions for alternative arrangements must be read against her general affirmation of the American tradition, so her sense of choosing her own style in child rearing was secured by her appreciation of her own childhood and her desire for motherhood, for she believed that these would protect her from destructive choices. She drew an immense freedom from her conviction that she had no inherent temptation to destruction and that the arrangements that best served her professional life, given her ingenuity, were in no inherent conflict with my welfare. Over the years this attitude was contrasted with cultural styles that depend upon a suspicion of one's own cruel or evil impulses, as English children are taught to be kind to animals because of the temptation of cruelty. *page 32*

Another scene of my childhood was the Museum of Natural History, which often served as a baby-sitter as soon as I had learned to find my way back up, after hours of solitary exploration, to the fifth floor. Indeed, everyone who succeeded in visiting Margaret in the museum arrived with a sense of achievement and discovery after trekking down echoing corridors of blank-faced storage cabinets that led to one more flight of stairs up to her tower office, nested beyond shelves and shelves of American Indian pottery and other specimens. This was an odyssey that might also involve convincing some guard who didn't know me that I was allowed in these restricted areas, and often I had to ask for help to find the right elevator or corridor.

Occasionally Margaret would bring me into the museum before opening time and leave me to wander off alone among the fixed tableaux of life in jungle or desert or deep in the sea, or would take me out through the darkened halls, haunted with ancient or alien lives, after closing time. Once she arranged for my birthday to bring a group of my friends into the preparation rooms, to see how the great dioramas are built. She daydreamed that my wedding could be held in the Hall of Pacific Birds, against the background of a great curved diorama of flamingos flying away into the sunset, but by the time I married the museum was no longer allowing the use of any of its spaces after hours for nonofficial functions. *pages 68–69*

Where Margaret always gave the culture in which she had grown up the benefit of the doubt, Gregory did not. He looked around at the American scene, seeing increasing corruption, and used the analogy of addiction—another form of regenerative feedback—to describe many activities and institutions. Much of Margaret's popularity with ordinary people has been based on the fact that she affirmed and respected their ways of doing things, their decencies and aspirations, even when she did not herself conform. Much of Gregory's popularity in the last decade of his life was with the counterculture, those who rejected contemporary forms. But behind his rejection was an appreciation of form and a demand for mental discipline that most of his followers did not acknowledge.

It was this, I think, that underlay Gregory's attraction to Zen Buddhism and made him hospitable to its extreme attention to formal detail, even though he always stayed at the periphery. There was also a congruity between his developing view of the sacred as immanent in the mental structure of the natural world and the immanent Buddhist sense of the sacred. He first started talking in the fifties about Zen training, in which insoluble problems are posed to the student, so that the attempt to hear the sound of one hand clapping might lead to enlightenment. He compared this process to the double bind where insoluble dilemmas are posed in the context of the key relationships of childhood and may lay the groundwork for schizophrenia, but saw similarities to humor and creativity. *page 97*

Over the years, conversations with my mother helped me to recognize these continuities and allowed me to stand back and think about what I was doing and why. Even so, as I look back over these sequences, it seems to me to have been critical that my path separated decisively from hers at an early stage, so that our conversations took place in a context of distance. The thing she was most afraid of as a parent was that her capacity to think herself into the lives of others, imagining possible futures, would lead her to guide me in a way I would later repudiate. In any quarrel between us, the thing that would have hurt her the most, because it had been said to her so many times, would have been to accuse her of dominating me or interfering with my life. This was a point of vulnerability so deep that we conspired to protect the relationship, she by refraining from advice and indeed by trying to restrain her imagination about me, I by carefully monitoring the kinds of indecision or uncertainty I shared with her. I learned to show my imagined futures to her only when they already had a degree of vividness that I could continue to acknowledge as my own, unable to say, this is your plan I have been living, your fantasy projected onto me. She had the capacity to live many lives, participating richly, reaching out in complex empathy, grasping hold of possibilities that had so far eluded the imagination of others, and so she had to monitor the dreams she dreamed for others. *pages 110–111*

My adult relationship with Gregory was in direct continuity with my childhood relationship—visits to him spaced out over time, focused in dialogue, sometimes embedded in the larger conversation of a conference in which we looked at or thought about some natural phenomenon or his own evolving ideas. The number of ideas was not large—he pursued a small set of highly abstract themes all his life, although the examples and parables used for teaching them changed more rapidly. It was possible to be away for a year or two and come back, stepping again into much the same deep and slowly moving river. Introverted and involuted, his thought is well described as a sort of incubation, and he was tolerant of those who came and went if they were interested in engaging with his ideas. Unlike Margaret, he used to try to draw me away from other kinds of involvement, and seemed to almost forget my existence when I was not with him. Suspecting most of what I did of being a waste of time, he used occasionally to propose the possibility that Barkev [my husband] and I might come and live nearby, so that he and I could work together on the development of abstract understanding. He would shake his head impatiently, like a horse tossing off flies, when I talked of other kinds of work and other places. *page 113*

For myself, it seems to me that like many children I set limits on my curiosity about my mother, freeing myself for the tasks of my own life. I have never tried to read all her writings and indeed have only read about half the books she published after I was an adult and an anthropological colleague—it was too important for me to acquire my own point of view. But she read everything I published, following the various literary magazines I worked on in school, sometimes reading several drafts, wading through a dissertation and through technical linguistic discussions as my interests slowly moved closer to hers. *pages 122–123*

The voices of my parents are still very much with me, for I hear their echo in so much that I see and encounter. They affirmed that what is most worth caring about is an interweaving of pattern going beyond any individual person, and their voices are blended now into the complex skein. It was difficult for me sometimes, as a child, to decode the differences and similarities and to pitch my own voice in harmony but yet distinct. The contained world of early childhood no longer exists, but my concerns remain similar to theirs and the analogies that bridge from the microcosm to the wider world continue, from Pere Village to New York, from the distorted communication of a schizophrenic family to the Pentagon. Finally, it is because of this play of analogy that I have felt that my own memories should be shared.

Margaret and Gregory are claimed by many people, not only by those who had an actual share in their lives, but by many others who never met them but have only read their writings or listened to a recorded voice or viewed an image on a screen. I find myself with a certain continuing responsibility for their writings and ideas, even as I acknowledge that my parents belonged to me no more than the photographs and records of my childhood, made in the specific so that someday that specificity could be projected out, an offering of enriching or clarifying models. *page 220*

Three years have passed since Gregory's death and almost five since Margaret's, but the legal estates are only barely through the complex process of settlement and Margaret's papers in the Library of Congress and Gregory's at the University of California at Santa Cruz are not yet fully catalogued. My father's final manuscript remains for me to complete as he wished,* and requests from biographers, textbook writers, and filmmakers continue to come in. I could easily devote myself full time to responding to these requests and to the claims of those who want some important project strengthened by being associated with my parents' names.

What then are the obligations laid on me by the rights that others feel they have? What do I do when the notorious star of a TV series decides that she was born to portray Margaret Mead on television, or when a magazine of New Age spirituality decides to write on Gregory Bateson's religious beliefs on the basis of a telephone interview with me? How do I respond to the biographers who assume that their interest in one of my parents gives them a natural right to my time? Do the ethics change when the second such writer comes along, or the third, and does it make a difference if they have studied anthropology or knew Margaret or Gregory in their lifetime? The second movie proposal? The third? And is it my task to deal with attacks and criticism as they come along, some of them constructive and some petty and destructive, when friends and relatives call late at night pouring forth their grief and anger?

The poem my mother wrote for me in 1947, began,

That I be not a restless ghost

Who haunts your footsteps as they pass . . . . *page 223*

---

* *Angels Fear* by Gregory Bateson and Mary Catherine Bateson (New York: Macmillan, 1988).

CHAPTER FOUR

Powerful Women: Mother, Great Grandmother

Betty Sue Flowers

An essay based on Betty Sue Flowers'
comments on "Texas Heroes: A Girl's
Point of View," presented October 28,
1984, at the symposium, Texas Myths: The
Personal and the Collective Mythology

Ralph Barrera

About Betty Sue Flowers

Betty Sue Flowers is professor of English at the University of Texas in Austin, where she graduated in 1969. She went on to take an M.A. in English. She received her Ph.D. from the University of London in England. In addition to teaching English, poetry and myth, Flowers is associate dean of the graduate school and the director, Plan II honors program in the College of Liberal Arts. A member of the Texas Committee for the Humanities, she is on the board of trustees of the Institute for the Humanities at Salado. She was born in Waco, Texas.

Author of the book *Browning and the Modern Tradition* (New York: Macmillan, 1976) and co-author of *Four Shields of Power* (Plainview Press, 1987), her edited books include *The Power of Myth, Joseph Campbell with Bill Moyers* (New York: Doubleday, 1988), *World of Ideas* with Bill Moyers (New York: Doubleday, Spring 1989), and *Daughters and Fathers*, co-edited with Lynda E. Boose (Baltimore: Johns Hopkins Press, 1988). Her articles include: "How to Make Fiction out of Your Friends," "The 'I' in Adrienne Rich," and "Madman, Architect, Carpenter, Judge: Roles and the Writing Process." In addition, she has published poems and short stories.

She has been a lecturer on Jacobean drama at Beaver College, London, and a research assistant in zoology at the University of Texas. In 1976 she was awarded the Andrew W. Mellon Fellowship at the Aspen Institute for Humanistic Studies, where she participated in executive seminars as co-moderator. In 1982 she participated in the PBS series, "Six Great Ideas," and in 1983 she won the Holloway Teaching Award at the University of Texas. Betty Sue Flowers is listed in *Who's Who of American Women; Directory of American Scholars; Contemporary Authors; The World Who's Who of Women; International Who's Who in Education;* and *Community Leaders of America.*

The journalist Molly Ivins is reported as saying that as a Texas girl, she had two role models—Bonnie Parker and Ma Ferguson. Growing up in Abilene, I knew of only one—Cynthia Ann Parker. The neighborhood kids played cowboys and Indians all summer long, and we never drew straws to see who would be cowboys. The boys got to be cowboys, and the girls got to be Indians—all the time. True to Texas myth, the cowboys always won, so I spent a lot of time during my formative years being captured and tied to the garage door. The only fun we girls had out of Texas myths was that we got to go "woo-woo-woo-woo" before we were captured. When I played Cynthia Ann Parker being rescued by the civilized whites, I didn't even get to whoop, but started off being tied up, and that wasn't much fun either.

Where were the folklorists when I needed them? If I had seen pictures of cowboys dancing in aprons, or if I had seen John Wayne just once playing the violin, we would have had some different games out there in Abilene.

We knew how Indians acted because we had all seen them in the movies. And we knew what the terrain was like from the movies, too. No matter that Abilene was flat and treeless—we landscaped our Indian wars with the buttes, canyons, and pine trees of southern California and occasionally threw in a few caves from *Tom Sawyer* for good measure.

The only powerful woman I knew from history, other than Dolly Madison, who saved the curtains and paintings from the White House, was Cleopatra. I didn't know much about her except that she sailed down the Nile in a barge and had Egyptian slaves fanning her and drank pearls dissolved in vinegar. Once I persuaded the neighborhood children to play Cleopatra—but the boys got tired of fanning me and started ducking arrows aimed at them from the hostile Indians along the Nile, and soon Cleopatra was captured and tied up again, just like Cynthia Ann. No one could figure out the rest of the story, so I stayed tied up a long time. Would the Texas Rangers rescue Cleopatra? What about her slaves? Would they help her or would they join the Nile Indians?

Of course her slaves would help her, I argued. After all, hadn't the effects of my great-great-great-grandfather, the Reverend Sam Corley, "sweet Singer of Israel" and the first Presbyterian minister in Texas, been brought home from the Civil War by one of his own slaves? And a slave who had already been freed? My great-grandmother told that story in a speech she gave at the Confederate Veterans reunion in Clarksville, Texas, when she was only 19:

> When honor and patriotism fired the soul of his noble master
> and called him forth to the gray field of battle, with courage
> undaunted this true-hearted servant willingly followed, ready

to serve him, if needs be, to die at his side. The great tide of civil war rolled on, leaving in its wake myriad mounds of cold gray earth until one morning in September of '63 during a skirmish with the enemy, this loved master fell mortally wounded. He fell into the hands of the enemy and was conveyed to a federal hospital where his soul, loosed from its earthly temple, took its flight to the country from whose bourn no traveler e'er returns. The servant never saw his master again, but crossing the federal lines he was allowed the privilege of a wagon and horse. Securing the master's horse and personal effects, he started with them back to the bereaved ones at home. Having dispatched this mission of love, he retraced his steps and delivering this wagon and horse to their owner returned once more to cast his lot with the children of his master. Nor did his faithfulness end here. He has also shown himself to be a friend of the strongest type to these children by deeds of kindness and self-sacrifice. That soldier was my grandfather and that servant is now a citizen among you.

I remember this same great-grandmother, sitting in her high-backed chair, quieting, with one syllable of her palsied voice, the Christmas babble of cousins and aunts and uncles and third-cousins twice-removed. Her oldest son, Great-Uncle Ben, leaned close to her and translated the mysterious sounds she made to the great-grandchildren. There was a real heroine, someone who would have saved not just paintings and curtains, but the White House itself, given half a chance. She had started the Shakespeare Club in Clarksville, so I read whatever I could of Shakespeare, including *Cleopatra*. Her other favorite book was the Bible, so I read the Bible cover to cover and came across that fierce woman Judith who tempted the enemy captain to lie down drunk and then chopped off his head. The Reverend Dallas Denver Denison of the First Methodist Church in Abilene never preached a sermon on Judith although I sat on the front row every Sunday for nine years waiting for some word about how a Christian heroine was supposed to act during cowboys and Indians or Israelites and Assyrians. Somehow I just didn't think Judith would have allowed herself to be tied up.

It was during the second year of the Rev. Denison's sermons that I decided I would grow up to be a boy rather than a girl. I had been taught one myth of the West which I took to heart—you can be anything you want to be if you work hard enough at it. So I played tackle football and wrestled down every boy on the block and hit homers, and when a little boy in second grade tried to kiss me, I socked him in the stomach so hard he went crying to the teacher, and I had to stay after school like all the other bullies. I ignored the films in the fourth grade which taught us girls that anatomy was destiny and so was totally unprepared for my initiation into the club of women, which came during the third quarter of a particularly brutal football game with only a few feet to go before we reached the castor-bean goal-line.

I wish I had known about Bonnie Parker or Ma Ferguson. I wish I'd known about Emily Morgan, the "Yellow Rose of Texas," who kept Santa Anna occupied in his tent at San Jacinto until Houston crept up on him, and he had to run away in red slippers and silk drawers. Maybe if I'd heard of Mollie Bailey, who ran a circus in Texas for fifty years, the neighborhood children could have thought to play circus once in a while. I would have loved to play Belle Starr, the Bandit Queen of Dallas, or Sarah Borginnis, "the Great Western," 6'2" tall and of such courage that at one battle she offered to wade across the Arroyo Colorado and whip the enemy with a stout pair of tongs.

Of course, Sarah Borginnis and the Yellow Rose of Texas were not proper role models for young ladies. The proper role model for girls was one's mother, who stayed indoors, even in summertime. There was a wide gap between indoors and outdoors. Indoors, neighborhood girls did chores, ironed and dusted and washed dishes. Outdoors, we were the Three Missketeers playing heroic games with the boys' gang, the Three Musketeers. The oldest Missketeer, Katherine Ann, was 12. Every day in the summer, the Musketeers and the two younger Missketeers would sit on Katherine Ann's concrete front porch in the shade behind the cannas and wait for her to finish the chores. Sometimes we came inside and joined her brother in watching the only television set in the neighborhood. Then, when Katherine Ann was finished with her chores, we would go outside and play cowboys and Indians.

We never played Alamo although we all knew the story well. The problem was, we didn't know how to play Mexicans. There were Mexicans (by which we meant Spanish-speaking people) in Abilene. And we knew they were supposed to be lazy and say *"mañana"* all the time. But how do lazy people who sit around all day under *sombreros* and play the guitar storm a fort? And what about casting? If the boys played Davy Crockett, they would have to lose to the girls . . . but only after killing 20 Mexicans apiece since the way the cowardly Mexicans had won in the first place, we all knew, was because there were so many of them. We just didn't have enough Missketeers for 20 of us to die at the hands of Davy Crockett and then enough be left over to go on to win.

Sometimes early in the morning before school started, we all gathered on the Lincoln Junior High playground to watch the Mexican boys fight each other. People said they were fighting because one of them tried to take the other one's girlfriend away—just like the real

Musketeers in the books, it seemed to me. When the patrol cars pulled up, and the rest of us ran with pounding hearts to the safety of the front steps, the Mexicans would keep right on fighting, for honor.

I knew about honor, and I knew that Yankees and Mexicans weren't supposed to have it. Texans had it at the Alamo and Confederates had it, and both had been defeated. In East Texas, the family would gather around the Christmas turkey and creamed corn and cornbread dressing and boiled custard and Nesselrode pudding and sing "Dixie," and everyone had to stand, just like at the football games when they played the "Star-Spangled Banner" over the loudspeakers. Then sometimes we would stay standing to sing a long song about how each of the states seceded in order—"First gallant South Carolina nobly took the stand/Then came Alabama who took her by the hand" and on and on until the last chorus of "All cast on high the Bonny Blue Flag which bears a single star," and then Bessie or Ola would come in with the hot rolls, and we could eat.

I couldn't fit the Blacks into the story either. I knew they had been on our side because they weren't Yankees, and I knew Bessie and Ola loved me. They had their own ways and their own side of town and their own churches and restrooms and water fountains. But if the Blacks were on our side, what was I supposed to think about Abraham Lincoln? I figured he must have been one of us because he was a good man who freed the slaves, but for some reason he got stuck on the other side.

Back home in Abilene, I thought maybe we could have Cleopatra free her slaves, and then they could help her fight the Indians. But no one wanted to play Cleopatra again. The Musketeers thought it was boring. You had to stay in a boat and duck instead of running and yelling and then stopping in your tracks and wheeling around clutching an arrow in your stomach and falling to the dust and rolling under the thin shade of a mesquite tree, where it was cooler, to grovel in a long, drawn-out, dying agony. The Missketeers finally broke up. I set up a doctor's shop in the garage with old bottles full of colored-water medicine and my mother's black purse for a doctor's bag. Cowboys could drag themselves into the garage to lie on the dog blanket and have their arrows removed so they could return to fight the by now completely imaginary Indians. My sister Linda Ruth organized a neighborhood wedding with herself as bride. And Katherine Ann ran away from home.

CHAPTER FIVE

The Power and Limitations of Parents

Jerome Kagan

Adapted from a lecture and discussion at the Institute for the Humanities at Salado, October 20, 1985.

About Jerome Kagan

Jerome Kagan, professor of human development at Harvard since 1964, has received many honors and awards for his work. He says, "My success has been aided by a combination of hard work, openness to new ideas, a readiness to discard beliefs that are proven invalid, a desire to nurture the growth of others, and belief in the beauty of ideas and the perfectibility of men."

In his lecture at the Salado Institute on October 20, 1985, Kagan discussed the mystery of human development and his discoveries concerning the power and limitations of parents in influencing their children's personalities. After revealing the historical basis for current attitudes, he indicated how his own attitudes have been changed by the data he has gathered in his laboratory and by his study of other cultures and of history. He discussed how the power of parent and child interactions and experiences in the home is tempered by societal and historical factors operating outside the home, and how a child's development is influenced by the relations between the values of society and the values of the family.

Dr. Kagan received his undergraduate degree from Rutgers in 1950, a Ph.D. from Yale in 1954, and an honorary M.A. from Harvard in 1964. He has served as an instructor in psychology at Ohio State University; as a research psychologist at the U.S. Army Hospital, West Point; and as the chairman of the department of psychology at the Fels Research Institute in Ohio.

He is the author, co-author, or editor of 12 books, with three more forthcoming. Among his books are: *Birth to Maturity* (New York: Wiley, 1962); *Child Development and Personality* (New York: Harper and Row, 1979); *Creativity and Learning* (Boston: Houghton Mifflin, 1967); *Un-*

derstanding Children (New York: Harcourt Brace Jovanovich, 1971); *Infancy* (Cambridge, Mass.: Harvard Press, 1978); *Growth of the Child* (New York: Norton, 1978); *The Second Year* (Cambridge, Mass.: Harvard Press, 1981); *The Nature of the Child* (New York: Basic Books, 1984); *The Second Year: The Emergence of Self-Awareness* (Cambridge, Mass.: Harvard University Press, 1986); *The Emergence of Morality in Young Children,* Editor (Chicago: University of Chicago Press, 1987); and *Unstable Ideas* (Cambridge, Mass.: Harvard Press, 1989).

Human development is a mystery of concern to all of us as citizens and as parents because we are human beings who develop. We care less about the truth of lasers or heavy water molecules. But when it comes to truths about us and how we develop, we care a great deal. We want certain ideas to be true, and we resist other conclusions.

During our historical era (Western society since about 1700), there has been a major change in our views of the family and child. One reason is that a large middle class could afford to relieve women from picking berries and gathering wood and could give them some leisure. As cities with a large middle class developed, three beliefs became strong and they are still with us, even stronger now than they were 300 years ago. One is that what happens in the family sets the course of a child's development early in life and what is done cannot be undone. The second is that love for the child is the most critical ingredient. And, in our century, that love should be physical and involve embracing and kissing the child. Third, the mother is seen as the central figure in the child's development. These three beliefs are about 300 years old, and although they might be true, the scientific evidence for their truth is meager. A petit jury would say, "Let's try these ideas in the court of science and see how true they are."

There are three important factors responsible for the growth of these beliefs:

One is the rise of industrialization and a larger middle class. Society did not need middle-class women to work but sought to give women a job that they believed was important. Society chose "raising the child." It could not have given them a more important assignment. As a result, the rise in the dignity of women, compared with other parts of the world, was enormous. In Europe and North America, women have enjoyed more dignity in this century than they have ever had in any society in the past.

A corollary of this increase in dignity (about which the historian Carl Degler of Stanford has written a wonderful book) is that love and affection were celebrated. Whenever a society enhances the importance of women, it also tends to emphasize the importance of love and affection.

The third factor is the Protestant tradition. One of Luther's important beliefs was that the mother was a central figure. This premise is an important part of the Protestant credo. Second, love in the family, not outside the family, is paramount. Luther was bothered by the high rate of adultery in the fifteenth century. He urged men to pick a wife who would be not only the mother of his children, but a love object as well. He emphasized that one must train character early and the task of early training belongs to the mother.

Those are some of the reasons for these beliefs. I held these beliefs as a young psychologist. Because of my training in college and graduate school and my political leanings, I was a devout environmentalist in my early work. When my daughter was born, I urged my wife to stay home so that she could give her a lot of love. What changed these beliefs were my observations—visiting other cultures and reading history. History permits one to see one's own culture in perspective. In rural Zaire, adults believe the mother should not be with her newborn infant, and women pass babies around. In parts of Polynesia, if a relative of a pregnant woman says to her, "I want your child when it's born," the mother cannot refuse because the request is a compliment. So the child is born, and at about age two, is given to the relative on another island. Attachment theory would regard the separation as cruel. But the Polynesian society is functioning. History and anthropology teach us that cultures practice what appear to us to be incorrect rituals. But they survive, and often their rates of psychosis, neurosis, and crime are less than ours.

Our traditional beliefs cannot be as true as they seem to us or as true as the magazines and books would have us believe. There are so many factors that influence the young child that even though maternal love and attachment have influence, it is less than common ideology claims.

Human development has two different stories to tell. One story asks the following question: What are the universal characteristics of human beings—the qualities that belong to all of us just because we inherit the genes for being human? We have language, apes do not. We experience guilt, shame, and pride, apes do not. Excluding the extreme case of a child raised in a closet or locked in a basement, human beings around the world will be very similar. How does that happen? This is of interest to a great many psychologists.

The second story is of more interest to parents and asks: How can we understand the differences among us? In textbooks this theme is called personality.

Psychologists have made important discoveries about the universals. For the universal qualities that belong to all children, the specific family constellation is less critical.

The best example is language. The brain of a newborn baby is immature. The fundamental structures in the brain are the neurons and synaptic connections. The brain of a newborn infant is about as mature as that of a rat, but its growth is not complete until adolescence. As the brain grows according to its genetic script, the infant becomes able to do certain things. A six-month-old child cannot understand language or speak no matter what one does because its brain is not mature. At about 13 months, the brain reaches a level of maturity that enables the child to use the experience of hearing speech to begin to speak. We say that the child is biologically prepared to learn language, as long as it hears language. The key words are "biologically prepared." We would use the same words for birdsong. We say the bird is biologically prepared to sing its song, if it hears it. If a canary, isolated and hatched in a laboratory, hears the song of a canary at the right time in its development, just for a few days, later it will sing its song. All it needs is a little bit of exposure.

Consider four examples of biological preparedness in children. First, at around eight to nine months of age, the human brain reaches an important milestone. Now the infant can remember the past. As adults we can remember what we had for breakfast, what we did yesterday at 9:00 A.M. But before eight months, infants cannot remember the past because their brains are not sufficiently mature to let them reach back and retrieve what happened 30 seconds ago. When they are eight months old, they can. Now they are vulnerable to becoming anxious. Have you ever noticed that older people who lose their recall memory become less anxious? A basic condition for anxiety is remembering the past and comparing it with the present. If the two ideas do not fit, one has a problem. And if one cannot solve that problem, one becomes anxious. A sputtering jet engine produces anxiety only in those who can remember how it ordinarily sounds. If one could not remember that sound, one would not become anxious.

At about eight months of age babies become afraid of strangers and of separation. At about eight or nine months they may cry if a parent leaves the house, but a four-month-old baby rarely cries to this event. The eight-month-old baby cries because as the mother leaves, it is able to compare that fact, the memory of her presence, with the fact that she is absent. The baby can't understand this. The eight-month-old has a problem: mother was present moments ago, but mother is not present now. And because it can't understand this, it becomes anxious. Infants become anxious at this time because of the growth of the brain.

A second preparedness involves our moral sense. The Tree of Knowledge allegory in the Bible was one of the wisest statements about human nature ever written. Remember that when Adam and Eve ate from the Tree of Knowledge, God made them different from all animals; they knew the difference between right and wrong. Most philosophers acknowledge that all humans have a moral sense.

But after the First World War, American psychology, in a rush of environmentalism, claimed that if a parent did not teach the child right from wrong, it would not know the difference. We taught our students those ideas in the 1930s and 1940s. But all children with an intact brain will, between the ages of about 17 and 24 months, become concerned with broken or flawed objects. This a time when the infant will look at its pajamas and because a thread is hanging say, "Mommy, look." A 12-month-old would not say that. The child between 17 and 24 months will see a cup with a little crack and say, "Fix it, broke Mommy, broke Mommy." If something is out of place, or if a toy is broken, the child becomes anxious, even though he or she did not misplace or break it. There is suddenly concern that the ideal form has been flawed. Where does this concern originate? Parents don't tell children, "The cup should not be cracked." This sense of the proper occurs by two years because the child is mature enough to recognize that there is an ideal and a nonideal form and that the ideal is the better. The child understands right and wrong events. This concern is as profound a competence as language.

A third ability which emerges is empathy. One of the important intellectual advances in early childhood is the ability to make an inference, especially about the internal state of another. At two years of age, if a child lives with other human beings, he or she can infer that a person or an animal might be suffering. David Hume called this emotion sympathy, psychologists call it empathy. Empathy for the state of another is a fundamental human emotion that does not have to be taught. Suppose a pair of two-year-olds are playing and one takes a toy away from the other, who cries. The face of the aggressor may become tense, and within a few minutes the aggressor will give a toy to the victim—a form of penance reflecting the aggressor's sense of having caused the other pain.

An encounter between a couple of two-and-half-year-old boys illustrates this ability to know the mind of the other. One was aggressive and kept pushing the other away, and in half an hour the victim was totally intimidated. There was a Batman costume in the playroom that was not being used. The victim took the Batman costume and put it on, and then saw that the aggressor wanted it. So the victim began to parade in front of his peer, showing off the Batman costume, and said, "That's okay. You can hate me if you want." This two-and-a-half-year-old child was able to infer jealousy in a child he had known for 30 minutes. Empathy, like the singing of birds and swimming of fish, is a prepared talent.

If a two-year-old child has empathy, and knows that he or she has caused the hurt, then guilt emerges as an emotion. Guilt, too, does not have to be taught. We are prepared to have a conscience. One mistake modern psychiatry made was to invent the term "psychopath" for a criminal who murders without emotion, implying that the person never had a conscience. As long as this person was not brain-damaged, at the age of two he or she knew right from wrong and was capable of empathy. Experiences after childhood dampened this ability. One can mute basic emotions—an analogy is love. If one is rejected in love many times, it becomes harder to fall in love again. Life experiences can blunt the capacity for empathy, too.

I believe that women in the West are more empathic then men, but this sex difference is not universal. Japanese men are very empathic. It is a tradition in Western society that men achieve and be autonomous and individualistic; women should be nurturing, protective, and healing. One can't be achieving, individualistic, and competitive if one is sorry for the victim. Western men must suppress empathy for their rivals or fail to accomplish their goals. There is a potentially serious problem among female executives in America because they find it difficult to fire people. It is harder for a woman than a man to hurt another. The most salient defining characteristic of women in our society is to avoid hurting another. Causing pain is the hardest thing for a woman to do. It is easier for men. That is a profound difference between the sexes, at least in our culture.

Piaget, one of the great psychologists of this century, believed that children pass through stages of development and that one important stage occurs at about six to seven years of age; in isolated, small villages it may occur a few years later. As a result of maturation of the brain, a new set of abilities emerges. One of the most important of these is that the child can compare self to others and understand that he or she is prettier, less brave, a better reader, or not as strong. A four-year-old child does not continually compare self with the larger group. Some believe there is a third-grade slump in school. In the first grade children are adapting to school, and it is hard to predict what will happen, but by the third year they have come to understand their relative talents, to decide whether they are good at this activity.

Of course, once one is able to understand where one fits in the larger group, an important part of the self-concept grows. For a child cannot know know how smart she or he is without looking around at the other children in the classroom.

Remember that the Catholic Church does not require confession before the age of seven; English common law, too, does not view a child as responsible for a crime prior to seven years of age. Long before there was anything called child psychology, citizens understood that something profound happens at age seven. In Guatemala, Indian parents who have eight or nine children and don't know their ages assign a boy the cutting of a new field of corn, or a girl the responsibility of caring for a younger sister. Children must give off some sign to their parents indicating, "I am now ready for responsibility."

A final preparedness occurs at adolescence when youths become able to examine their beliefs as a whole and detect inconsistencies. If a set of beliefs is inconsistent, they become troubled. An eight-year-old boy can hold the following two beliefs and not feel uneasy: "My father is a wonderful man," and "My father yells at my mother." A 13-year-old cannot help but sense the inconsistency and must resolve it. Adolescents are able to detect that some beliefs—about God, sex, family, future— don't necessarily fit logically. They become troubled. The tensions and stress of adolescence have less to do with sex hormones than with the ability to recognize personal beliefs that don't fit. This tension is more salient in the West than in small, closed communities around the world where everybody in the village has the same set of beliefs. Where there is little inconsistency, adolescence is a less troubling time, much less troubling than in Western societies where there is so little consensus on basic premises.

These qualities develop because, as human beings, we are prepared for their actualization.

Turning now to personality, how can we account for the differences among children or adults? First, let us decide what qualities to consider. Each culture values a small number of qualities, a few ideas it cares about. Four qualities we care about are: first, technical abilities—some children are smarter than others, some are better at machinery, some better with words. Second, we care about differential wealth and status—some have a lot of status, dignity, and power; others have little; and we wonder why. Third, we want to know why some people have successful social relationships and family lives because we believe that friends, love, marriage, and family are important. Finally, since we have become a sensate society, we want to know why some people are happy and some are sad. We want to know why these differences in personality exist. Depending upon which one is selected, the mix of influential forces will be different.

Six factors influence differences in ability, status, wealth, social ties, and happiness. Depending upon which factor one picks, the balance will be different. It would be presumptuous to suggest that the six forces explain everything, but they are important. But only for one of them does a parent have complete power.

The first factor of influence is the biological temperament of the child. Those who have had more than one child or grandchild know that babies are different from the moment they are born. These differences are partly genetic and partly prenatal. Babies differ in how active they are, how irritable, how easily they adapt to a schedule. One quality we are currently studying involves reactivity to unfamiliarity and challenge.

If Jung were alive he would smile because he believed introversion and extroversion were two of the most fundamental personality dimensions. The quality we are studying is related to these dimensions. In the first two years of life, some infants are fearful, cautious, and shy. If a stranger comes into the house, they rush to their mother. If taken to the doctor, they cry. In nursery school they don't let their mothers leave them, and the mother sometimes has to stay several weeks before such a child will permit her to leave. Perhaps 10 to 15 percent of all children are born with this quality (of course, one can also make a child shy through family experiences). Another 15 percent are born with a bias to be bold, fearless, and outgoing. It is very hard to frighten them.

Over a period of six months we brought 400 children to our laboratory and observed them in various situations. About 10 to 15 percent were consistently shy and timid, while another 10 to 15 percent were bold and outgoing.

But parents of very timid, frightened children who are gentle in promoting change can gradually make a difference; about half of our timid children are now neither shy nor timid. Although it is possible to influence this quality, many families don't try. Many parents are fatalistic about their children—"That's the way he [or she] is, and it'll be okay." By the time they enter school these children are shy. If they come from middle-class homes where schoolwork is valued, they may choose an intellectual career. T. S. Eliot, for example, was a timid, shy child who remained an anxious man throughout most of his life.

A second influence on personality is birth order. Is a child firstborn, secondborn, or thirdborn? (I am referring to differences for a thousand firstborns versus a thousand later-borns. Consequences do not apply to each individual.) Among middle-class Americans, the firstborn is generally more responsible, gets better grades, makes more money, goes to a better college, and commits fewer crimes. When stress occurs, the firstborn is less likely to become very distressed. Those born later are more likely to develop problems; they tend to be more pragmatic, less idealistic, and more likely to be rebellious.

In an interesting book called *The Promised Seed*, Irving Harris examined famous firstborns and later-borns and showed that the rebels and terrorists of the world are more often later-born; thinkers and idealists are more often firstborns. Trotsky was a later-born, Marx a firstborn.

To the firstborn in a traditional middle-class home, the world seems orderly. Parents are nurturing, predictable people who set high standards and are kind. The world is a just place, wherein if you do what you're told, everything will be fine. When firstborns venture into the world, they ask of their parents, "What is it that you want me to do? Be a scholar? A businessman? Fine. I will do what you wish." The firstborn is trusting, idealistic, and works hard.

But imagine you are a later-born with a firstborn brother who is unpredictable. When you talk to him, he doesn't always reply. He seizes toys from you and hits you now and then. The firstborn is allowed to stay up until 10:00 while you have to go to bed earlier. The world looks a little less fair and these conditions continue for years.

Thus, we might predict that firstborns would be more concerned with adhering to social order and have less propensity to disagree with authority. One would expect them to promote harmony, be less hostile and rebellious. We would predict that if a theory threatened many members of society, the later-borns would be more likely to favor it. I refer to brilliant discoveries that people care about. Citizens cared when Copernicus and Darwin said that the Bible was wrong, while the laser, although an important discovery, didn't threaten our beliefs about humans in society.

A young historian named Frank Sulloway took 13 ideological revolutionary figures in science, including Copernicus, Francis Bacon, Freud, and Darwin. In the *Dictionary of Scientific Biography* he discovered which eminent scientists in the ten-year period around a particular discovery said about the idea—were they for or against it—and correlated this with whether they were first- or later-born. He found that a majority of the scientists who said, "That's a good idea," were later-born men, while a majority of those who opposed the ideas were firstborn. The scientists' attitudes to a new discovery had less to do with what their parents might have done to them than with their ordinal relationships to their siblings.

I don't know if later-born children in other societies have experiences similar to those of the West; there is no research on ordinal position and psychological qualities in these other societies. But if the theory holds in Mexico there should be more firstborns with good grades in school. The classic Chinese family has been large, but because of a desire to limit the population, it is now illegal to have more than one child. The Chinese are upset because the personality emerging in these only children is more selfish and narcissistic than they would like.

A third influence on personality is what parents do to the child. This is most important in the first six years of life. There are three things that parents do which have a profound influence in their children. One of the least impeachable facts about the early years of life is that providing a lot of variety for an infant will facilitate the child's mental development. That is a reliable fact in a field with few facts. Parents who play with their children and talk to them, present them with tameable variety will promote mental development. Obviously, the adult can be a babysitter or staff member at a day-care center. Variety works. Indeed, one can tell the difference between a working-class and a middle-class child by two years of age. Although working-class mothers love their children, they tend to provide them with less variety.

A second way parents influence their children is through praise and punishment. As everyone's grandmother knows, a child learns values this way. If parents praise academic work, their children will be more concerned with doing well in school, at least temporarily.

Finally, in our society today, parents have to communicate to the children that they value them. Why "in our society today?" We all have a moral sense, thus, we evaluate events as good or bad and ourselves as good or bad. We want a gentle conscience. When all is quiet, the day's work is done, we ask ourselves, "How are you doing?" We want to be able to answer, "I am a good person." The man who wrote *I'm Okay, You're Okay* was trying to say the same thing. "I'm okay," means "I'm good." Essentially humans are moral creatures engaged in a moral mission.

If a child grows up in a third-world village and has to gather wood for the family or wash clothes in the river, parents don't have to tell the child he or she is loved because it is obvious to the child that he or she is good. The child is aware of making a contribution to the family. No one has to say "I love you very much, Maria"; Maria knows she is of value. But in our society, where children make no economic contribution to the family, they need to be told that they are good. That is why love—a communication of value—has become important. History has made it important.

One task in life is to persuade ourselves that we are good—morally virtuous. Our virtue is obvious if what we are doing is helping our family. It is good for a child to feel that he or she is useful. But affluent parents can't say, "Please do the ironing," because the child can say, "You can take it to the laundry."

A lot of children in the first and second grade have problems learning to read, but there is not enough money in school systems to hire special teachers. High school juniors and seniors who have the right personality and conscientiousness can tutor first- and second-grade children. Not only would this help the first and second graders, but the adolescents would feel virtuous doing something beneficial and useful. There would be a considerable dividend, and the cost would be trivial; I would like to see this experiment tried in several large cities and evaluated.

Although American parents should communicate to their children that they are valued, physical affection is not required. John Stuart Mill regarded his father as wonderful, but noted that he was not an emotionally expressive man. In his autobiography, an emeritus colleague, George Homans, writes, "I could not have been blessed with a better father. I always enjoyed being with him. I respected him. Yet I must say, I never felt emotionally close to him." One can feel loved and love one's parents even though there is little physical affection. Young people have a hard time understanding this idea because our contemporary culture equates parental love with embraces.

Fifteen years ago when I was working in Yellow Springs, Ohio, a pediatrician called me because the police had discovered a three-year-old child whose psychotic mother had locked her in a room. The child had a kidney problem, and her urine had an odd odor. She was mute and disturbed. Her mother thought the child was bewitched. The child was taken to a kind home and began to recover. I wanted to see what had happened to her, so I went back to Ohio when she was 15. She was doing well: the point of this story is love. I asked her, "Debbie, why do you think your mother did that to you?" Her voice was sincere as she said, "Well, you know, Momma had a lot of children. There were four of us, and I was a lot of trouble. That's why she did it." As far as she was concerned, she had a wonderful mother, even though she knew that her mother had locked her in her room for three years. Children are forgiving!

Puritan parents who loved their children beat them to tame their wills. There is a wonderful autobiography by a Reverend Wayland.

When his son was 18 months old, the father locked him in a closet because the child refused a piece of bread. Three hours later his father opened the closet, offered the bread to the child, and the child refused it again. He was shut in the closet for another 18 hours. If that happened today, we would call the police. But that is how Puritan parents "trained character." This boy ended up a respected citizen and president of Brown University, and probably loved his father.

If the prevailing cultural definition of love requires physical affection, then, of course, parents must adhere to that definition; if they don't, their children will wonder why the girl next door gets a lot of physical affection and they do not. A child is vulnerable to what the culture decides is the sign of affection. There are societies in which no one kisses children, yet they feel loved.

The fourth influence on personality is, in my opinion, the most important: the technical word in psychology is "identification." A child believes that the qualities of its parents are its own. Thinking "I have the last name of my family. I have the same hair color as my father, and my aunt noticed that we both have a funny dimple," the child goes beyond that evidence and concludes, "My father's popular, I must be popular. My father's talented, I must be talented." Or, "No one respects my father, and so no one will respect me."

One of the most important influences on a child is contained in what parents are as role models. Most parents have a hard time hiding their qualities. If a seven-year-old girl perceives her parent as competent, kind, nurturing, and attractive, she will feel much better about herself than she would otherwise. If a parent is incompetent, unpopular, and perceived to be mean or unjust, the child, despite having done nothing wrong, will feel guilty. Schizophrenics often feel they had a bad, rejecting mother; a prototypical statement made by a young schizophrenic is: "I'll tell you the problem, Doctor, deep down inside me there is a great deal of evil." This is the result of identification with a parent whom the child perceived as rejecting.

One can also identify with one's social class. If a child is a member of a minority group and perceives the group to be rejected, then he or she has a problem. In our society, some Hispanics and Blacks are troubled because even though they may be successful as adults, they identified with their class when they were young. A moving book written by John Edgar Wiedeman tells the story of a pair of black boys who grew up in a ghetto in Pittsburgh. The older brother, a professor of English at the University of Wyoming, has written several novels and is well-respected. The younger brother is serving life for murder. Wiedeman, himself the older brother, tries to come to terms with this in his book,

Brothers and Keepers. He writes that even though he is a professor of English, an author, and a respected member of his community, every morning when he wakes up he is afraid people will find him out. It must have been hard to write that sentence, which is the product of an identification. Wiedeman's belief that someday people will discover that he's not very good reveals how powerful an identification with a class or ethnic group can be.

How long does the parent remain a role model? In healthy development the child of four becomes sensitive to the personal qualities of his or her parents and is able to identify with them. By 12 years of age, children should be able to evaluate themselves on their own. At that point, if undesirable things happen to the role model, the child will not always take it to heart. But the identification sometimes remains strong, as depicted in *Death of a Salesman*. When the grown son Biff discovers that his father, who was his hero, is a man with clay feet, he is both anxious and angry. Here Arthur Miller portrayed the power of the identification of a young adult, although Biff should have been past this stage.

The fifth influence on personality is environmental success and failure. Success in school, for example, is a function of the size of the school. There are studies showing that if talent is held constant, the odds of a child being successful are better in a small school than in a large school. Some children are popular, some are not. My colleague George Homans was not very popular; he has written that, bullied and teased, he decided he would be good in school. That decision was determined in part by his unpopularity with the other boys. It had less to do with his parents than with his peer group.

The last factor in personality is chance. Unlike the Chinese, Malaysians, or Koreans, we in the West are unwilling to acknowledge the role of chance. The Greeks acknowledged the role of the gods. In the *Odyssey* Athena decides what will happen to Odysseus: maybe she will cause a storm, maybe she will set his ship on the rocks. The Greeks understood that chance is important. But in the West we want to believe that we are masters of our own fate. If we are successful or if we fail, we did it. And in our theories of development we do not assign power to chance.

Consider something outside of anyone's control, such as the size of the town in which a child grows up. According to *Who's Who in America* for 1985, although a majority of Americans live in urban areas, a majority of those in *Who's Who* grew up in towns with a population under 100,000. Consider a hypothetical girl with an IQ of 120 who is attractive and has loving parents. If she lives in Salado, Texas, there will be few girls as talented as she, and she will graduate from high school full of self-confidence because she compares herself with the other girls in the town. In Chicago, there would be many more talented than she and she would learn humility. Most of the first group of astronaut candidates grew up in small towns, towns without a museum, an aquarium, or excellent science facilities. To succeed dramatically it helps to have the illusion that one is better than others. A child does not have that illusion if there are hundreds of children who are more talented. But the place of rearing is a chance event.

Another chance factor is societal events like the Depression of 1930–1935. Sociologists have found that those who were between 7 and 15 years of age during the Depression were profoundly influenced. Many adults in Europe during World War I, the "spiritual war" that was to solve the world's problems, became skeptics. In this country, those in high school during the Vietnam War were profoundly influenced. My daughter was a sophomore in high school at that time, and the Vietnam War influenced her entire class. In her class there was a very talented girl who, one week before going off to college, wired the university that she wasn't coming and married a waiter instead. Five years earlier that would not have happened. And, of course, the Vietnam War had nothing to do with how good or bad a set of parents each child had. Similarly, those between the ages of 7 and 15 today will be profoundly influenced by the introduction of computers into the school.

We live in a larger framework. For reasons that are beyond our control, the economy, social structure, industrialization, and mobility of our society requires individualism. Our society has carried individualism too far. There is too little caring and cooperation. But a change in the balance can occur only at the level of the entire society. For example, a former student of mine was a pacifist and believed that his firstborn son should not be punished. He and his wife intended to raise their son to be cooperative and to turn the other cheek. For the first few years he was a beautiful boy, but then it was time for nursery school. He went off to a good nursery school. Two months later the teacher called and told the parents that the boy was being bullied and would not hit back. So they had to change their strategy.

It is possible to have an effect through changing institutions within society. If, for example, a large number of American schools celebrated the student who contributes to the community as much as the valedictorian, there would be a change. But we also need cooperation from professional schools.

It is possible we are becoming a more sensitive society. If we take the short view, given the headlines about hijackers and the poisoning of our lakes, it may seem that times have never been worse. But take the long view. Western society has steadily enhanced the value of the individual human life. If someone in Manitoba were killed by a kidnapper, it might be on the front page of the *Boston Globe*. That would not have happened a hundred years ago. We care more about individual lives. We are revulsed by violence and believe every life is sacred.

To summarize, six factors have profound effects on children. Only two involve parents—what they do and their function as role models. Thus parents have power, but their power is limited. Humans are prepared by nature to believe that they can have an effect on the world, and one should be conscientious as a parent and reflect on one's actions. But we must realize that the growth of a child is monitored by many factors, including temperament, historical era, and birth order. A life is the complex story with numerous collaborations.

There was a rabbit, sitting in the forest, typing. A dog came up and said, "Rabbit, what are you doing?" The rabbit said, "I'm typing a story." The dog said, "Well, what's the title?" *"Rabbit Eats Dog."* The dog said, "Well, that's impossible." The rabbit said, "You come with me," and they went into a cave. Ten minutes later the rabbit came out, licking his chops. Then a wolf came by, and the wolf said, "Rabbit, what are you doing?" "I'm typing a story." "What's the title?" *"Rabbit Eats Wolf."* "Oh," the wolf says," that's not possible." "You come back with me." Ten minutes later, out came the rabbit, licking his chops. Then a bear came by. The bear said, "What are you doing, Rabbit?" Rabbit said, "I'm typing a story." "What's the title?" *"Rabbit Eats Bear."* "Aw," he said, "you're kidding me." "You come back with me." Ten minutes later out came the rabbit and a lion, licking their chops. The moral of this story is that it's not the title of your story that is important, it's who your collaborators are.

References

Degler, C. 1980. *At Odds: Women and the Families in America from the Revolution to the Present.* New York: Oxford University Press.

Harris, I. 1964. *The Promised Seed: A Comparative Study of Eminent First and Later Sons.* New York: Free Press of Glencoe.

Homans, G. C. 1984. *Coming to My Senses.* New Brunswick, N.J.: Transaction Books.

Mill, J. S. 1879. *A System of Logic, Ratiocinative and Induction.* 8th ed. 2 vols. New York: Harper.

Sulloway, F. 1972. "Family Constellations, Sibling Rivalry, and Scientific Revolutions." Unpublished manuscript.

Wiedeman, J. E. 1984. *Brothers and Keepers.* New York: Holt, Rinehart, and Winston.

Excerpts from *The Nature of the Child*

Indeed, nineteenth-century European and American authors were concerned more with the mother's emotional involvement with the baby than with the baby's attachment to the parent. In an essay on motherhood, Elizabeth Evans wrote, "The strongest human tie, is, understandably, that which binds a mother to her child" (1875, p. 7): but nowhere in this 129-page essay did its author ever say that the infant naturally binds itself to the mother. The famous German psychologist William Stern also questioned the intensity of the infant's attachment: "How quickly the little child gets used to a new nurse, even when it had great affection for her predecessor; how little the child misses—perhaps after short pain at parting—its parents when they leave home or a favorite animal." *page 53*

Although many nineteenth-century observers would have understood and probably agreed with Bowlby, few would have written three books on the theme of attachment because, like the blue of the sky, the idea was obviously true. Bowlby's conclusions are newsworthy in the last half of the twentieth century because historical events have led many citizens to question the inevitability of maternal devotion to the child and of the child's love for the family. Parental abuse and adolescent homicide of parents have undermined the nineteenth-century faith in the naturalness of familial love. Modern citizens have begun to question the universality of deep affection and continued loyalty, whether between adults or between parents and children, are saddened by the conclusions implied by that inquiry, and are eager to hear a wise commentator on human nature assert that the love between child and parent is an absolute requisite for psychological health.

There are good reasons why Americans in this century have become concerned with the potential hazards of childhood anxiety. First, the geographical mobility that increased in the United States after the First World War forced many Americans to live in communities of strangers whom they could not trust. Second, the combination of an economic depression, the atrocities of the Second World War, and later, possible nuclear catastrophe created in the average citizen serious apprehension about the future. I suggest that these uncertainties have been projected onto the infant. *pages 55–56*

Morality will always be a critical human concern because humans want to believe there is a more and a less virtuous outcome in a situation of choice, and therefore insist on criteria for action. The fact that two-year-olds are concerned with the correctness or the incorrectness of an action implies the primacy of this theme. Humans are driven to invent moral criteria, as newly hatched turtles move toward water and moths toward light. The conditions for moral virtue in modern society—the state that one seeks to attain in order to reassure oneself of one's goodness—include pleasure, wealth, fame, power, autonomy, mastery, nurturance, kindness, love, honesty, work, sincerity, and belief in one's freedom. Each is a construction built over time, though traceable to universal affects. The relative prominence of each of these values is not an inevitable product of the human genome, but stems rather from the capacity for empathy with another's distress, shame and guilt over violating standards, and preparedness to inhibit actions that provoke disapproval. These are not inconsistent views. The young child is prepared by his biology to become attached to his parents; yet Western culture insists that he eventually develop autonomy and independence from them and be able to cope with distress in their absence—qualities that not only require subjugation of the earlier natural disposition but also ones that are probably not biologically inevitable. The moral sense of children is highly canalized because of a capacity for evaluation and the experience of certain emotions, but the surface ethics of a specific community are built from a web of social facts embedded in folk theory. Although humans do not seem to be specially programmed for a particular profile of moral missions, they are prepared to invent and believe in some ethical mission. Par Lagerkvist had God reply to a question regarding His intention in creating human beings with, "I only intend that you need never be content with nothing." *pages 152–153*

While most intelligent children are not necessarily creative, most creative children are intelligent. But their creativity is based on three other characteristics: they have a mental set to search for the unusual; they take delight in generating novel ideas; and they are not unduly apprehensive about making mistakes. A major hallmark of the creative person is some indifference to the humiliation that can follow a mistake. This attitude gives the child freedom to attempt mental experiments that may fail and to consider high-risk solutions without worrying too much about their potential failure. *page 222*

In the modern Western world, the individual, not the family, is slowly becoming the basic unit. The high divorce rate, the large number of single-parent families, and the public's willingness to work toward a more egalitarian society through interventions that abrogate the family's power make the person the central entity in the eyes of the law, the school, and the self. Additionally, early socialization practices that promote autonomy, and individual, rather than group, effort and responsibility, lead many adolescents to conclude that their future mood and material success depend upon their personal abilities and motivation. A divorced woman with only a high school education who was living with her three-year-old said, "I must develop myself, I can't be dependent on anyone but me." This attitude may be historically unique. Although historians argue about the form of the earliest families and when the nuclear structure emerged, no anthropologist or historian has ever suggested that the majority of adults living in older societies believed that their survival, personal reputation, and material success did not depend primarily on their family of rearing. Thus, each American adult must acquire a special state of mind which most families, consciously or unconsciously, train for from the earliest months of life. Few citizens of ancient Athens, Babylon, or Jerusalem, or of modern Tokyo, Jakarta, or Beijing (Peking) would understand this attitude. Thus, some of the qualities of the modern Western family are specific to this historical era. *page 243*

The belief that the emotions experienced repeatedly during infancy are preserved is attractive to parents and social scientists. But this outcome is not inevitable. Older children who have experienced a great deal of uncertainty during the opening two or three years of life do not always become distressed adolescents, especially if their environments become benevolent after the period of infancy. A twenty-seven-year-old woman who had been abused continually as an infant, and had lived in three foster homes before she was three years old, managed to convince herself during adolescence that she was not inherently bad. She became a loving, satisfied mother who was deeply identified with her only son. By contrast, adult Mayan Indian men living in small villages in northwest Guatemala are hostile, suspicious, and aggressive toward their wives, despite a secure attachment to their mothers who nursed them on demand and stayed close to them for most of the day.

I am not suggesting that it is irrelevant how adults care for infants. It does matter! But an insecure attachment during the first year need not always lead to adult pathology, and a secure attachment is no guarantee of future invulnerability to distress. If a secure attachment motivates the child to adopt characteristics that are maladaptive in the larger society, as can happen during periods of transition when old values are changing, the attachment might not be beneficial for the child. Children living in Bombay have a secure attachment to mothers who are playful, caring and loving. Nonetheless, many contemporary Indian adolescents are anxious because new cultural demands are inconsistent with the values they adopted earlier as a result of their close attachment to their mother. An infant girl in Boston who is closely attached to a mother who promotes passivity, dependence, inhibition of intellectual curiosity, and excessive sexual modesty will grow up possessing qualities that are not adaptive for women in modern America.

Infants need variety of experience and opportunities to explore and to manipulate their environment in order for cognitive development to proceed optimally. To develop a secure attachment, they need a consistently nurturant adult who regularly relieves distress. The consequences of these benevolent experiences, however, will depend on the demands that the social environments make upon the child in the future. There is no way to inoculate the infant against adult misery, even though parents might be able to make that mood a little less probable. *page 254*

. . . the five-year-old must believe she is valued by her family. This belief is not an obvious derivative of the state of attachment established during infancy. I have noted that Western society attributes considerable power to parental love, and has done so since the seventeenth century. The psychological power ascribed to parental love, or its absence, has a parallel in the potency attributed in other societies at other times to spirits, loss of soul, sorcery, sin, gossip, God, and witchcraft. "Parental love" has two meanings. One refers to the special emotion parents feel toward a child. A second refers to the child's belief regarding the favor in which he or she is held by the parents. Western society is preoccupied with the significance of the first—a mother's feeling of love for her young child—and assumes that the child's belief will follow automatically. But these two meanings are not always correlated. Experts warn of the potential danger of diluting the mother–child attachment with substitute caregivers. The film *Autumn Sonata* (1978) provokes private assent from hushed audiences who hear a married woman tell her aging mother that the former's psychic anguish is a historical transformation of the mother's failure to love her thirty years earlier. A mother's love for the child is treated as a mysterious force which, if sprinkled plentifully over young children, guarantees salvation. But for the child who is not fortunate enough to have had a loving mother, the future is poisoned. If most human societies held this belief, one might be persuaded of its validity; all people believe that one must eat to survive. But the contemporary Western belief in the long-lasting psychological danger of insufficient maternal love is not shared by many societies, nor was it held by our own society several centuries ago. *pages 265–266*

My own image of a life is that of a traveler whose knapsack is slowly filled with doubts, dogma, and desires during the first dozen years. Each traveler spends the adult years trying to empty the heavy load in the knapsack until he or she can confront the opportunities that are present in each fresh day. Some adults approach this state; most carry their collection of uncertainties, prejudices, and frustrated wishes into middle and old age trying to prove what must remain uncertain while raging wildly at ghosts. *page 280*

PART II

THE MOTHER
THE FATHER

CHAPTER SIX

The Eternal Woman: The Worship of Mary in Art

Elizabeth Silverthorne

An essay prepared at the request of the Institute for the Humanities and written following Ms. Silverthorne's trip to Europe to study Mariolatry in art.

About Elizabeth Silverthorne

Elizabeth Silverthorne is a free lance writer who resides in Salado, Texas. A graduate of Texas Women's University and North Texas State University, her career experiences have been diverse. She has taught at North Texas State University and Temple Junior College and spends her spare time in travel and research. She is a member of the board of trustees of the Institute for the Humanities at Salado.

Silverthorne's publications include a number of short stories, articles, and books. Among her book titles are *The Ghost of Padre Island* (Abingdon Press, 1975), reprinted in *My Weekly Reader* in 1976; *First Ladies of Texas* (coauthored, Stillhouse Hollow Press, 1976); *I, Heracles* (Abingdon Press, 1978); *Ashbel Smith of Texas* (Texas A & M University Press, 1982), which won awards from the Texas State Historical Association, the Daughters of the Republic of Texas, and the Sons of the Republic of Texas; *Plantation Life in Texas* (Texas A & M University Press, 1986), winner of four awards from historical societies; and most recently *Marjorie Kinnan Rawlings: Sojourner at Cross Creek* (New York: Overlook Press, 1988).

The roots of Mariolatry go back as far as primitive man and as deep as man's yearning for a female divinity who will protect and nurture him and whom he can worship and love.

Bludgeoned by the more strident elements of the feminist movement, many males struggle today to reconcile their ambivalent feelings toward women, between whose thighs they both receive and create life. From ancient times men have wrestled with the problem of separating their sometimes lustful, sometimes worshipful, feelings about their biological complements.

Almost all early religions had goddesses of fertility, and since the characteristics connected with these mother images were often gross, perverted, or hazy, it is something of a miracle that they could be converted into the chaste, benign, tender image of the Christian Madonna. But there is good evidence that in every land where the Madonna came to be worshipped, the foundation had been laid by some previous idea of a mother goddess, one who represented a kind of divine maternity.

In her popular works of fiction about the first inhabitants of Europe, Jean Auel shows the worship of an Earth Mother connected with water. Recent discoveries in Egypt have led to revelations of a vast animal cult dating at least to the 26th Dynasty. The bull was worshipped as a symbol of strength and fertility, and it was the custom to choose a new sacred bull, or Apis, when the old one died. Isis, the mother of Apis, was also worshipped as being fertilized by a divine spirit, thus establishing the cult of the virgin cow.

In other cultures, Isis was identified as having been originally a rustic corn-goddess. In *The Golden Bough,* Sir George Frazer devotes three long chapters to a discussion of the goddess connected with the decay and revival of vegetation, beginning with the myth of Demeter and Persephone. He points out that their story is essentially the same as that of Aphrodite and Adonis from Syria, Cybele and Attis from Phrygia, and Isis and Osiris from Egypt. There are numerous examples of harvest customs in Europe—some still practiced—that call for a ritual involving the last of the crop, which is supposed to contain the spirit of the grain and is called such names as The Maiden, The Old Wife, The Great Mother, Corn-Mother, Rice-Mother, Harvest Mother, and others. Greek and Roman artists represented Isis with ears of corn on her head or in her hand.

Whatever her beginnings, Isis eventually evolved into the serene, dignified, and saintly goddess who was worshipped throughout the Roman Empire and in many other countries far from her native land of Egypt. Her influence and her various guises are best described in her own words:

> I am she that is the natural mother of all things, mistress and governess of all the elements, the initial progeny of worlds, chief of the powers divine, queen of all that are in hell, the principal of them that dwell in heaven, manifested alone and under one form of all the gods and goddesses. At my will the planets of the sky, the wholesome winds of the seas, and the lamentable silences of hell are disposed; my name, my divinity is adored throughout the world, in divers manners, in variable customs, and by many names. (Campbell 1971b, p. 56)

The declaration goes on and in the middle of it, Isis sums up the various names she is called, including Minerva by the Athenians, Venus by the Cyprians, Diana by the Cretans, Proserpine by the Sicilians, Ceres by the Eleusinians. But, she complains, only the Ethiopians and the Egyptians call her by her true name—Queen Isis. She concludes by mentioning the benefits she provides for her worshippers:

> Behold I am come to take pity of thy fortune and tribulation, behold I am present to favor and aid thee; leave off thy weeping and lamentation, put away all thy sorrow, for behold the healthful day which is ordained by my providence. (Ibid.)

In the Roman Catholic Litany of Loreto addressed to the Virgin Mary, all of Isis's attributes are transferred to Mary, who is termed the Mother of Good Counsel, Virgin Most Powerful, Virgin Most Merciful, Seat of Wisdom, Cause of Our Joy, Gate of Heaven, Morning Star, Health of the Sick, Comforter of the Afflicted, and Queen of Peace.

Another striking similarity between the two heavenly queens can be seen in the statue of a throned Isis nursing her infant son Horus and the many representations of Mary enthroned and nursing her infant son Jesus. Scholars have compared the Christian legend of the Holy Ghost, which, in the form of a dove, causes Mary to conceive through the ear her Holy Son, who was born in a cave, died and was resurrected and is recalled in the communion service through the use of bread and wine to the legend from ancient mythology in which Zeus appears in the form of a serpent to his own daughter Persephone (another name for Isis) and causes her to conceive his son Dionysus, who is born in a cave, dies, and is resurrected and known as the god of bread and wine. Persephone, as well as being a fertility goddess, is the queen of the lower world ruled by Hades (Campbell 1971a, pp. 27–28).

Another example of the dual deities with whom Isis identifies herself is Astarte, the Assyrian goddess who was both the lover and destroyer of men. Again her name changes as we cross the borders of different countries, but she is frequently referred to as Ashtoreth and as Ishtar. Those who worshipped her called her Woman of Women, Mother of the World, Kind Mother, and You Who Prolong Life. In one of Plautus's plays, a character addresses her as "Divine Astarte, source of strength, life and health, destruction and carnage." Statuettes show her, like Diana, to be many breasted, symbolizing her fertile life-giving attribute. Her lover and son by virgin birth was Tammuz, who died yearly and was born again—at her insistence. Rituals of prostitution and castration were regularly performed as a part of her worship. Astarte is identified as a heavenly goddess who gave birth to the sun regularly on the 25th of December. This birth ritual, connected with the winter solstice, came to be represented by the image of an infant.

Another ancient goddess, who like Astarte had a dual nature, and who underwent physical changes corresponding to that nature, is the Hawaiian deity Pele. Sometimes she appeared as a destroyer and sometimes as a loving preserver. She symbolized youth, beauty, and love and as the preserver of life gave the people water in time of drought and food in time of famine. When they did not treat her with the proper respect, she erupted in the form of a volcano and "ate the land." When she appeared by the seashore, she was old and ugly, but on the volcano top she was young and beautiful. The prayers of the Hawaiians to Pele for immortality are similar to those in the Roman Catholic liturgies to the Virgin Mary.

Early Celtic worshippers often named their rivers, lakes, hills, plains, and mountains after goddesses, whom they gave the collective title of Matronae. These Celtic divinities were connected with fertility and sovereignty, and they became the embodiment of the powers of death and life. Their sculpted figures often appear in groups of three, carrying baskets of fruit, cornucopias, babies, and other objects that symbolize their connection to earthly and human fecundity.

Endless examples of these earth- or mother-goddesses could be given, for as Joseph Campbell, lifelong scholar of mythologies, points out:

> It is simply a fact . . . that the mythology of the mother of the dead and resurrected god has been known for milleniums to the neolithic and post-neolithic Levant. . . . And so it came to pass that, in the end . . . Mary, Queen of Martyrs, became the sole inheritor of all the names and forms, sorrows, joys and consolations of the goddess-mother in the Western World: Seat of Wisdom . . . Vessel of Honor . . . Mystical Rose . . . House of Gold . . . Gate of Heaven . . . Queen of Angels . . . Queen of Peace. (Campbell 1971a, pp. 44–45)

Henry Adams, who thought that the proper study of mankind should be of women, made a penetrating analysis of the sculpture and iconography of Chartres Cathedral in order to present evidence that the Virgin Mary in the twelfth century emerged as the last and greatest of the mother-goddesses. He believed that the scientific mind atrophies when it comes into contact with "the eternal woman—Astarte, Isis, Demeter, Aphrodite, and the last and greatest deity of all, the Virgin." Adams claimed that only an artist could understand this eternal woman. The implication is that if ordinary mortals hope to gain insight into her, they must study the ways in which artists have treated her.

It is unlikely that Judea produced any art pertaining to Mary during her lifetime, since Hebrews forbade images of all kinds. It is also doubtful that there was any religious art for some time after the death of Jesus because of the persecution of the early Christians. The first supposedly authentic portrait of the Virgin was one described by a number of writers as having been in the possession of Pulcheria, the extremely pious sister of the Roman emperor Theodosius II, who ruled from 408 to 450.

The most ancient representations extant of the Virgin in art are those on the Christian sarcophagi and in the catacombs, dating from not later than the third or fourth centuries. There is an image of the Virgin holding the Child on her lap in the Catacomb of Priscilla at Rome. These pictures are done in the style and technique of ancient Roman wall paintings, but it is obvious that in this case the artists were not interested in painting beautiful pictures. Their aim was to remind the viewers of Christian ideas. In the Catacomb of St. Ciriaco is painted a woman with arms outstretched, evidently representing Mary as a Madonna of Witness. The same figure is repeated frequently on the sarcophagi with slight variations.

If we accept the Edict of Milan in 313 as the decree that allowed Christians freedom to worship, then this is also the date when Christian art was free to come up from the tombs and the catacombs into the light of day. Byzantine artists began to display a passion for portraying the Virgin Mary with the baby Jesus, always seeming to strive for a superhuman majesty, posing the elongated bodies of their figures stiffly. A common technique was to portray the Christ Child as an old man in miniature in an attempt to convey his wisdom. This practice disappeared only when the humanistic approach in art developed.

In the fifth century, Nestorius and his followers began to teach theories that undermined the idea of Mary's divinity. They maintained that the title "Mother of God" was not proper because in Christ the two natures, God and man, remained separate and Mary was parent of the man, but not of the god. In 431 the Council of Ephesus met in the same city in Asia Minor that had been for millenniums before the coming of Christianity the chief temple site of the great Asian goddess Artemis, "Mother of the World and of the Ever-Dying Resurrected God." The Council condemned Nestorius and his party as heretics, and representations of the Madonna and Child became an expression of orthodox faith—hung on the walls of houses, embroidered on garments, carved into furniture, and worn as personal ornament as well as used profusely in the churches.

An icon dating from the sixth or seventh century (St. Katerina Monastery, Mt. Sinai) is a good example of the best of the work of the early Christian artists. It shows the Madonna and Christ Child in a tender, serene mood with a strong suggestion of other worldliness about it. The encaustic technique of mixing pigment with melted wax gives a convincing sense of modeling to the figures. Typically, both figures are given an air of sanctity by the use of halos.

The veneration of the Virgin in the early Irish Church is shown in an illumination from the late-eighth-century Book of Kells. The picture, which shows Mary seated holding a long-haired, mature-looking child, sparkles like jewelry with a profusion of ornament. She wears a stylized halo that has the appearance of a jeweled crown. Writhing, fantastic serpentine forms encircle the couple, bringing to mind God's mandate in Genesis that the seed of woman shall bruise the head of the serpent, who in turn shall bruise the heel of the offspring.

In the ninth century the effigy of the Virgin began to appear on Greek coins, replacing earlier pictures of Athena and other mythological representations. The Virgin often appears on these coins, veiled and draped, in the act of crowning the emperor.

In the twelfth century, Marian art reflected the early beginnings of a new trend toward realism and grace. Manuscript illumination was one of the most characteristic arts during the twelfth and thirteenth centuries, and in the British Museum *The Enthroned Madonna* can be found in a manuscript psalter. A contemporary of the Vierge Doree at Amiens, in it, too, the mother gazes directly at her child and appears more human than in earlier images.

The great cathedrals of Europe provide the most striking example of Christian art, and the many that were dedicated to *notre dame* in France during the Middle Ages show the attitude of the people toward the Virgin. The cathedral at Chartres is one of the best examples of the loving care and craftsmanship that went into creating these dwellings for the Holy Mother. The survival of the original Royal Portal, unscathed in the great fire of 1194 that burned the rest of the church, is considered one of several miracles performed by the Virgin at Chartres. Over the right-hand doorway of this portal Mary is shown in several scenes. In the nativity she lies on a low bed beneath a cradle, illustrating her ability to understand the human pain of labor and birth. The Virgin's mother, St. Anne, is portrayed a number of times in the church, reminding worshippers of the divine birth of Mary herself and of the royal lineage of Christ.

Above the north transept of the church is the huge Rose of France with the Virgin seated majestically, crowned and holding the scepter in her right hand, while her left supports the infant Jesus. Around her in a circle are 12 medallions, all symbolizing the gifts and endowments of the Queen of Heaven. The art of creating stained glass reached its peak in the period when these windows were completed. The walls of shimmering, colored light were thought to symbolize the true word of God, and the way light is transmuted by stained glass was compared to the process of the incarnation and virgin birth of Jesus. The ideals surrounding the twelfth-century cult of the adoration of the Virgin evolved the codes that have come to be known as courtly love and chivalry. In the twelfth and thirteenth centuries Ovid's *Art of Love* circulated both in Latin and in the vernaculars. Without questioning Ovid's sincerity, the upper classes took many of his ideas and combined them with ideas about religious love to form the basis of a new system of behavior connected with male–female relationships. Under the influence of the veneration of the Virgin, the troubadours of southern France modified these ideas. A granddaughter of one of the troubadours, Eleanor of Aquitaine, was responsible for introducing these ideas on courtly love into the north of France. As in the religious teachings concerning the Virgin, the ennobling effect of love upon the lover is repeatedly emphasized in connection with knighthood and chivalry.

In the Middle Ages, thousands of men enrolled in brotherhoods, such as the Carthusian, Cistercian, and Carmelite orders, devoted to Mary's especial service and to acts of charity performed in her name. In a world where life was short and full of misery for the average man and where the specters of sickness and death were his constant companions, it is little wonder that he preferred to let his thoughts dwell on a better life in another world and on the tenderness and beauty of the gentle Virgin who might intercede for him in heaven. In the churches and monasteries icons of the Virgin often appeared below images of Christ to emphasize her role as the mediator between God and the congregation. The idea of Mary as intercessor was particularly appealing and enduring. In the early twentieth century, communists in Mexico who tried to debunk Mary's importance found that the faith of the half-starved, disease-ridden peasants in their compassionate Virgin was stronger than any political lure that could be offered them.

As literacy and literature developed in the Western world, hundreds and thousands of prayers, poems, and hymns were written to the Virgin by monks and devout scholars. The sacred and the profane were often blended in the many Middle English lyrics dedicated to Mary's praise. Sometimes she was praised as the new Eve. Frankness and humor enlivened the devotional lyrics, and they expressed wonder at the virgin birth. In "I Syng of a Maiden," one of the best known of these lyrics, the poet concludes with the paradox (from Spencer, et al. 1974):

> Moder and maiden
> Was never non but she;
> Wel may swych a lady
> Godes moder be.

In addition to the poetry, numerous prose stories of Mary's appearance on earth and of the miracles she performed were recorded. Caesar of Heisterbach recounts her assistance to a knight who was delayed in getting to a tournament because he stayed too long praying to Mary in a chapel. Mary took his place and won the victory for him. Minerva herself could not have done better.

The miracle plays of the Middle Ages show Mary's role as an intercessor with her often severe son. The foolish virgins in the *Play of the Wise and Foolish Virgins* seek mercy from God in vain. Then they turn to the Virgin Mary, saying (from Schaff 1964, p. 838):

> Since God our suit hath now denied
> We Mary pray, the gentle maid,
> The Mother of Compassion,
> To pity us, sinners poor, to pray
> Mercy from her beloved Son.

Various episodes in the life of the Virgin provide subject matter for a number of the mystery plays also. Three plays in the *Ludus Coventriae* deal with the Conception and the early life of the Virgin. The subject matter derives ultimately from three of the apocryphal gospels, which were well known in the Middle Ages. According to these gospels, Anna and Joachim long for a child and believe their barrenness is a sign of God's rejection. When, after much lamenting, they are told by an angel that Mary will be born to them, their despair turns to joy. The second play shows Mary being presented at the temple at the age of three. Her meditations as she ascends each step make up the heart of the play. The third play in the cycle is episodic but presents an interesting viewpoint in that it stresses Joseph's age and shows his reluctance to wed Mary. He says, "But I am so Agyd and so olde that both myn leggys gyn to folde." And he worries about their future: "An old man may nevyr thryff/With a szonge wyff so god me save." Finally Joseph accepts God's will with reverence (Woolf 1972, pp. 160–162).

Other mystery plays that specifically concern the Virgin deal with the Annunciation, Joseph's doubts about Mary's pregnancy (quite frankly and even obscenely expressed), the visit of Mary to Elizabeth, the Nativity, the adoration of the shepherds, the adoration of the Magi, and the death and assumption of the Virgin.

Quite obviously connected with Mariolatry is the attitude of the two great Italian poets Dante and Petrarch toward their idealized women. Both of them raised their earthly loves almost to the level of goddesses. Petrarch lifts Laura to a plane of spiritual worship and reveres her as his divine guide to a better world after death (from Mack, ed. 1965, p. 1189):

> Oh, may she deign to stand at my bedside
> When I come to die; and may she call to me
> and draw me to her in the blessed place!

Dante's *Divine Comedy* revealed and influenced the medieval mind as no other work did. In both this poem and in *New Life,* he praises Beatrice's physical beauty as much as her spiritual qualities until (he says) she finds it necessary to instruct him to keep his thoughts away from sensuous ideas. A strict hierarchical order is maintained throughout the *Divine Comedy,* and thus Beatrice, blessed as she is, cannot accompany the poet into the exalted realm where Mary dwells.

When Dante finally sees Mary, he is unable to put her beauty into words, and in the words he does use there is some implication of physical attraction:

> I saw the virgin smile, whose raptures shot
> Joy through the eyes of all that blessed throng;
> And even did the words that I possess
> Equal imagination, I should not
> Dare, the attempt her faintest charms to express.
> *Paradiso,* Canto XXXI

Dante's contemporary and friend, Giotto, expressed the same duality of feeling about the Virgin in his paintings of her. By comparing his enthroned Madonna with that of his teacher Cimabue, we can see how radically Giotto cut the ties to the old Byzantine tradition of painting Mary primarily as a symbol. In his *Lamentation* her face is that of a flesh-and-blood mother, distorted by anguish as she bends over her dead son.

This breakthrough of the barriers of symbolic representations of the Virgin opened up new possibilities that many other artists continued to develop. Some of the ideas attached to the worship of Venus became associated with the worship of Mary, and divine and human elements were fused as in Botticelli's *Birth of Venus*. It has often been noted that Botticelli's Venus has the same wistful innocence and the same aloof gaze as his Madonnas. However, there were those who disagreed violently with the artists' attempts to combine the divine and human elements, especially when it was done in paintings of the Virgin. And Savonarola, the leader of the protesters, influenced Botticelli to destroy many of his "too realistic" paintings of the Virgin.

The three titans of the High Renaissance in Italy—Leonardo da Vinci, Michelangelo, and Raphael—revealed in their treatment of the Virgin the unique qualities that set them apart from their contemporaries. Leonardo took the naturalism of the fifteenth century and combined it with a new spiritual expression in *The Adoration of the Magi* (Uffizi, Florence). His Virgin is not confined to a throne, but is seated on a bank in the open air. Although there are many figures in the picture, the important ones are made to stand out by the use of lighter colors and their arrangement in a pyramidal design. The impression the picture gives viewers is that they are watching a group of people who are under a spell of love for the new-born child so tenderly held by his mother. In his two versions of the *Virgin of the Rocks* (Louvre and National Gallery, London) Leonardo seems to combine the mysteries of nature with the mysteries of religion. The figures are in a grotto, which exudes a mist that envelops the group in an intimate, mystical, dreamlike atmosphere. Also in the National Gallery in London is Leonardo's famous cartoon of the Virgin and Child with St. Anne and St. John the Baptist, in which human beauty and a mother's tender love combine dramatically with supreme spiritual passion.

Since Michelangelo even in his paintings is under the influence of his skill as a sculptor, it is in his statues of the Virgin that we best see his contribution to Madonna art. While he was working on his *David*, he carved a statue called *Madonna and Child*. The relationship between the two figures is unconventional in that the child is standing between his mother's knees rather than seated on her lap or held in her arms. The Virgin's draperies reveal the anatomy beneath their folds. The faces are solemn and thoughtful and deliberately subordinated to the bodies as expressive features.

Michelangelo's progress toward his ideal of "the plastic expression of ideas solely by means of the human form" can be seen by comparing his early *Madonna and Child* with the *Virgin and Child* in the Medici Chapel in S. Lorenzo in Florence. The movement of the figures has become more complex. The Virgin's right shoulder is forced back, while her head is turned to the left. Her legs are crossed, and the Child is astride them, his body twisted sharply as he searches for his mother's breast. The face of the Virgin is again less important than the body, and the drapery is used only to delineate the underlying form. The dualism of body and spirit give his figures unusual poignancy. His philosophy of statues as bodies released from their marble prisons, and the body as the earthly prison of the soul, may account for the fact that his outwardly calm figures seem to be bursting with unreleased energy.

The two Pietas (the suffering Virgin) that Michelangelo did at the beginning and at the end of his career also show a dramatic change in technique and purpose. In the early *Pieta* in St. Peters, he is a virtuoso (although only 23 years of age) using his skill and knowledge of the human form to create a masterpiece. This Virgin is the epitome of the sorrowing mothers. In the Rondanini *Pieta* which he was working on shortly before his death, the wraithlike figures seem to go back to a medieval spiritualism. It is as if Michelangelo was doing this work to satisfy some private, deeply felt religious yearning known only to himself.

Raphael, the third of the trio of great Italian High Renaissance painters, was much influenced by the other two. When he went to Florence and found that the quiet style he had learned under his teacher, Perugino, had been outdated by the dramatic force of the works of Leonardo and Michelangelo, he was quick to absorb their most outstanding qualities. His new style evolved as a synthesis of his own genius plus Leonardo's pictorial ability and Michelangelo's sculptural instinct.

Raphael is best known for his paintings of the Madonna and Child. They are admired for their dignity and serenity and are totally different from the sweet and sentimental Madonnas of the earlier Italian masters. In two of Raphael's early Madonnas, the *Alba Madonna* and the *Madonna of the Goldfinch,* the restraint and nobility of the figures echo Michelangelo; and the pyramidal structure and shading to create an atmosphere are reminiscent of Leonardo.

Raphael's *Sistine Madonna* is characteristic of the High Renaissance in its monumental treatment of the figures and in the subordination of the background. The figures are grouped in a pyramid with the Virgin at its peak set against a cloud of tiny cherub heads. On either side she is balanced by the figures of Pope Sixtus and St. Barbara. The folds of the

Pope's robe, the billowing drapery of the Virgin's veil, the downcast eyes of St. Barbara, and the upward gaze of the saucy cherubs carry the eye in a circle and give rhythm and cadence to the picture.

The Venetian painters of the High Renaissance reflect the love of warm, sensuous colors, light, and drama that characterized the city and its citizens. Titian's painting *The Assumption of the Virgin* is heroic, full of energy and action. After he was 90, Titian produced his *Madonna and Child*. The picture shows the child nursing as his mother holds him tenderly and watches him somberly, as though aware of his destiny even as he draws life from her.

In northern Europe several important painters used the Madonna theme. The Van Eycks, in the Netherlands, introduced a method of oil painting that opened up a new era in art. Jan Van Eyck's skill in the use of color, space, and light is shown in his picture *The Madonna and Child*, in which sunlight streams in through a window to light the faces of the Virgin and Child.

Germany had close ties to Italy, but her artists developed their own version of the Renaissance style. Dürer, the northern counterpart of Leonardo, follows the realistic tradition in his painting *Virgin and Child with St. Anne*, in which he uses figures obviously those of a German grandmother, mother, and child.

With the Reformation came a decline of interest in religious paintings. Newly formed Protestant groups particularly disliked Madonna art as being too strongly Catholic in its orientation. Some artists, however, continued to use conventional religious subjects, giving them a new and sometimes shocking treatment. In his most famous work, *The Madonna with the Long Neck*, Parmigianino shows the influence of Raphael, but he has elongated the ivory-smooth limbs of his languorous Mary until she is as unreal as the early Byzantine representations of her.

Throughout the years, artists continued to portray Mary realistically or symbolically according to their beliefs and purposes. Most of these representations can be grouped under the five themes that have been used since the beginning of Marian art:

1. Ave Maria, the young Virgin before the birth of Jesus. Most of the paintings of the Annunciation are of this type. Mary is depicted with a girlish face, showing innocence, joy, humility, and sometimes bewilderment—as in Rossetti's *Annunciation*. In this painting Mary sits drawn up on a narrow bed while an angel done after one of Rossetti's friends hands her a stalk of lilies. Mary, modeled by the artist's sister Christina Rossetti, is stunned and wide-eyed. The effect on the viewer is that of a miracle happening before one's eyes.

2. Mater Amabilis, the young mother adoring the child. These pictures show the tenderness of the young mother toward the child by her expression, her gestures, or her actions, such as nursing or teaching him. Often a radiant light seems to come from the infant and is reflected in the mother's face. The nativity paintings fit into this group as do those showing the adoration of the child by the Magi or the shepherds. El Greco, who lived during the time of the Counter-Reformation, painted a *Nativity* in which a supernatural light radiates from the child, flashing from object to object and transforming the Virgin's face from that of its Spanish model to that of the Holy Mother.

3. Madonna of Witness, mother and child fulfilling their mission. In these representations the Madonna is often enthroned, and both she and the child are turned to the viewer. They are not absorbed in each other as in the nativity scenes. Cimabue and Giotto used this theme as did Botticelli and Raphael. In the *Madonna with Chancellor Rolin,* Jan Van Eyck used it to please his patron-donor and to create a small masterpiece of symbolism.

4. Mater Dolorosa, the grieving mother. Many anonymous church carvings are of this type, as are the crucifixion representations in which Mary appears. All of the Pietas belong to this group. Surrealist Salvador Dali presents Christ and the Virgin as modern figures in his version of the crucifixion. Nevertheless, in spite of the fact that Mary's hair might have been done by a modern hairdresser and her robe designed by Dior, Dali has captured the agony and loneliness of the bereft mother.

5. Regina Coeli, Mary, Queen of Heaven. Paintings or sculpture of the Assumption and of the Coronation fit into this classification. Mary may wear a halo of light, a halo studded with stars, or a crown; or she may be in the process of being crowned, as in Botticelli's *Coronation of the Virgin.* Rubens combined the energy and opulence that characterized the Baroque period in a painting depicting the Assumption of the Virgin.

In the twentieth century two important sculptors have used the Madonna as a subject. In 1927 Sir Jacob Epstein carved a large sculpture of a Madonna and Child on the facade of the Convent of the Holy Child, Cavendish Square, London. It is made of stone and has great size, power, dignity, and simplicity. The feet point downward as in a Byzantine mosaic, and the Virgin's draperies are reminiscent of Greek statuary.

Another Britisher, Henry Moore, has done a Madonna and child in stone for the Church of St. Matthew, Northhampton. The figures, fused in the massive style that is his trademark, seem to exude quiet and strength and a sense of compassion.

Hundreds of other artists and craftsmen—writers, painters, sculptors, musicians, architects, stained-glass artisans, wood-carvers, glassblowers, potters, metalworkers—have indulged in Marian art. Some makers of icons connected with the Madonna have no doubt been influenced purely by expectation of monetary gain. Others have used their skill and Mariolatry chiefly as a means of displaying their talent. But many have created their interpretations of the Virgin as an expression of their deepest religious feelings. Clearly Mariolatry has been responsible for a great number of artistic masterpieces.

Like Dante and Petrarch, later poets often wrote poems in praise of the Madonna. Wordsworth, Browning, Longfellow, and Poe are only a few of the many illustrious poets who have used her as a theme. It was Shelley who wrote:

> See where she stands! a mortal shape endued
> With love, and life, and light, and diety;
> The Motion which may change but cannot die;
> An image of some bright eternity;
> A shadow of some golden dream: a splendour
> Leaving the third sphere pilotless.
> "Epipsychidion," Percy Bysshe Shelley

As he wrote these lines expressing man's eternal yearning for a female divinity of love and life and light, the poet might have been looking at a painting of the Virgin Mary by one of the great masters—or he might have been standing before a statue of Isis.

References

Adams, Henry. 1961. *Mont-Saint-Michel and Chartres*. New York: The New American of World Literature.

Campbell, Joseph. 1971a. *The Masks of God: Occidental Mythology*. New York: Viking.

_____. 1971b. *The Masks of God: Primitive Mythology*. New York: Viking.

_____. 1972. *The Masks of God: Oriental Mythology*. New York: Viking.

Capellanus, Andreas. 1941. *The Art of Courtly Love*. Translated by John Jay Parry. New York: Columbia University Press.

Cavander Kenneth. 1971. "The Astarte Phenomenon." *Horizon* (Spring 1971): 15–18, 27.

Clark, Thomas Curtis. 1941. *Poems for Life*. Chicago: Willett, Clark and Co.

Duby, George. 1967. *The Making of the Christian West*. Cleveland: World Publishing Co.

Frazer, Sir James George. 1963. *The Golden Bough*. New York: Macmillan Co.

Friendly, Alfred. 1973. "Search for Tomb in Egypt Uncovers Vast Animal Cult." *Smithsonian* (August 1973): 66–72.

Gallagher, Sharon. 1969. *Medieval Art*. New York: Tudor Publishing Co.

Gibbons, James Cardinal. 1917. *The Faith of Our Fathers*. New York: P. J. Kenedy and Sons.

Gombrich, E. H. 1944. *The Story of Art*. London: Phaidon Press Ltd.

Highet, Gilbert. 1957. *The Classical Tradition*. New York: Oxford University Press.

Huyghe, Rene, ed. 1958. *Larousse Encyclopedia of Byzantine and Medieval Art*. New York: Prometheus Press.

Janson, H. W. 1952. *History of Art*. New York: Harry N. Abrams, Inc.

Levey, Michael. 1972. *Guide to the National Gallery*. London: Publications Dept., National Gallery.

MacCana, Proinsias. 1970. *Celtic Mythology*. London: The Hamlyn Publishing Group, Ltd.

Mack, Maynard, ed. 1965. *World Masterpieces*. New York: W. W. Norton Co.

Maus, Cynthia Pearl. 1947. *The World's Great Madonnas*. New York: Harper and Brothers.

Miller, Hugh. 1958. *An Historical Introduction to Modern Philosophy*. New York: Macmillan Co.

"Neoplatonism." *Encyclopaedia Britannica*, 1965, XVI, 217–220.

"Nestorius," *Encyclopaedia Britannica*, 1965, XVI, 253–54.

Newton, Eric and William Neil. 1966. *2000 Years of Christian Art*. New York: Harper and Row.

Painter, Sidney. 1953. *Medieval Society*. Ithaca, N.Y.: Cornell University Press.

Pettit, Rhea Ferne. 1970. *The Madonna Story*. Montezuma, Iowa: Sutherland Co.

Satin, Joseph. 1969. *The Humanities Handbook*. New York: Holt, Rinehart and Winston.

Schaff, Philip. 1964. *History of the Christian Church*. New York: Charles Scribner's.

Spencer, Hazelton, Beverly J. Layman, and David Ferry, eds. 1974. *British Literature*, vol. 1. Boston: D. C. Heath and Co.

Weigand, Hermann J. 1956. *Courtly Love in Arthurian France and Germany*, XVII of *University of North Carolina Studies in the Germanic Languages and Literatures*. Frederic Coenen, ed. Chapel Hill, N.C.: The University of North Carolina Press.

Woolf, Rosemary. 1972. *The English Mystery Plays*. Los Angeles: University of California Press.

CHAPTER SEVEN

Mother and Daughter Relationships

Mary Briner

Prepared by Mary Briner at the request of the Institute for the Humanities at Salado and adapted from her seminars on "The Psychological Aspects of the Mother-Daughter Relationship" at the C. G. Jung Institute, Zürich and Küsnacht. Mary Briner, an American Jungian analyst, lives in Kilchberg, Switzerland.

About Mary Briner

Mary Briner is a lecturer and training analyst at the C. G. Jung Institute, Zürich. Born in the United States and a graduate of Smith, she married a Swissman and moved to Switzerland. Living abroad poses many difficulties for American wives, among them housekeeping, education, and integration with the native culture. In response to these problems, Briner became active in founding the American Women's Club of Zürich. Seeing the need for cooperation with other American women's clubs in Europe, she took a leading part in the founding and growth of the Federation of American Women's Clubs Overseas, FAWCO.

During World War II she worked for the OSS under Allen Dulles. By war's end FAWCO no longer existed, its president dead following her internment in a concentration camp and all the records destroyed. Mary Briner undertook the responsibility of gathering surviving FAWCO members at a reorganizational meeting in Copenhagen in October, 1949.

FAWCO's initial goal of building bridges of understanding among nations has now expanded to include working for American citizens abroad concerning voting, citizen rights, taxes, etc. Mary Briner became its first postwar president, and the now thriving organization numbers thousands of women in its 35 member clubs worldwide.

Before moving to Zürich she had been interested in Jungian psychology and was therefore pleased to find herself living across the lake from Professor Jung. She attended the Vision and Zarathustra seminars in the 1930s. Professor Jung was her analyst, and she worked also with Mrs. Jung and Toni Wolff. She was one of the seven Zürich graduates who founded the Association of Graduate Analytical Psychologists of the C. G. Jung Institute in 1954. Mary Briner is also a member of the Swiss

Society for Analytical Psychology, on whose executive board she has served. She is still active in the C. G. Jung Institute, Zürich.

The mother–daughter relationship is one of the most vital of all human relationships, resolving itself into the relationship each woman has not only to her mother, but also to her own feminine psyche. The mother, or the mother image, is at least a determining factor, if not *the* determining factor, in a woman's relationship to herself as a woman—and particularly to her instinctive side. This inner attitude is reflected in the outer relationship both to her mother and in turn to her daughter. But most important is the inner relationship—the relationship between the mother and daughter within her. This mother–daughter aspect of the feminine psyche is determined by three factors. First, she is born with her own feminine structure. For just as we have a type structure—feeling, sensation, thinking, and intuition—so too, women seem to have a psychological structure of feminine functioning. Second, there is the cultural pattern of her time and country. Within its framework she will be influenced by education and any changes that occur in the masculine–feminine patterns. Here we find the influence of public opinion, of what tradition expects of a woman, of her conventional role. This is fertile ground for the animus, her contrasexual side. Third, the influence of her own individual mother and how it is constellated in her life affects the daughter. The mother–daughter relationship colors, or even distorts, the two other factors.

All women are daughters, but not all women become mothers—and some who do never become mothers psychologically. Nonetheless, the capacity for motherhood is nature's primary gift to woman—and it determines her functioning in the order of things. Regardless of what she does with nature's gift, it is woman's distinguishing characteristic. In each and every woman, there is always present the daughter from whom she cannot escape and the potential mother from whom she cannot escape psychologically. The mother represents the maturity of the daughter. When a daughter becomes a mother, then she is no longer a child, but grown up (or she should be), as if this were the goal of nature. I shall discuss the psychological goal later.

The biological function of reproduction has far-reaching and inescapable consequences for the lives of women because it is at this level that the instincts function. In modern times consciousness has undermined instinctive reactions, while the rational tries to eliminate the irrational. We no longer need to "feel" storms coming ahead of time when we can simply turn on the weather report. Nonetheless many vital decisions and actions in our lives are still conditioned by our instincts and their corresponding archetypes. The biological function drives us to the maturity we are meant to have.

Most women have a better relationship to their bodies than men do, despite the loosening of the instinctive connection. Women can accept bodily functioning, blood, and suffering more naturally, like animals, without fear—unless they are very neurotic. Yet I have never seen a woman with a difficult mother whose own body was not a problem. I wonder if the different psychological relationship that women have to their bodies does not have its roots in the very nature of those bodies: their ability to bear children and the accompanying menstruation.

In a split between instinct and consciousness the relationship to the mother is vital because it determines how well a woman tolerates this split. It is through the mother that women first contact their feminine nature and consciousness. Whether this contact is positive and supporting or negative and destructive can change a woman's fate. Many women are divided between home, children, and domestic life including relationship to a man, and work, career, and their own development. This double life with its demands from both sides can create conflict for women; but the problem is by no means limited to married women, for an unmarried woman's relationship to her instincts and her feminine consciousness is equally important to her life and fate. The problem of feminine consciousness is especially the *bête noire* of the "animus woman," who frequently has a negative mother.

How the modern woman copes with this problem is fascinating. Involved are the past and present attitudes of each woman to her own mother, and consequently her own attitude to herself as a woman, and the mother image as it is changing in the world. The mother of today does not seem to pass on to her daughter what we are wont to call the old-fashioned values of womanhood and so it becomes a collective problem for most women, with the archetype of the great mother in its broadest sense lying behind it.

It is doubly difficult for women to find a new point of view, for we have no archetypal feminine pattern in our culture or tradition to guide us. We have no goddesses who reveal themselves to us and differentiate women's nature. So each one of us has to experiment, seeking our own path.

Today this shows itself in the struggle of women to free themselves from the bonds of domestication in which many feel that the role of mother and housewife keeps them imprisoned. A woman must also struggle against being imprisoned by man's anima projections onto her. Thus, both the instinctive and traditional sides are in conflict with something else struggling to come to life within her.

How does she handle this practically in her everyday life? One woman told me that she wanted a full-time job and to be only a part-time mother. Another gifted woman said she would sacrifice all her outside activities if they in any way endangered her home and marriage. But the trend seems to be for women to be not *just* wife and mother, dissatisfied and frustrated, even if they want to be married more than anything else.

Woman's position has been in transition since the upheaval of forces which culminated in the French Revolution and the Age of Enlightenment at the end of the eighteenth century. At the same time there have been changes in man and his needs. The pace of modern life demands earning a living in a competitive and tough world. Men need help. Economic demands are forcing women out of the home even as pressure upon women to change comes from the natural process of growth within.

Woman's position is still in a state of confusion and no one seems to be quite clear about it—not even women themselves. Perhaps it is a matter of consciousness, and there is still a great deal to be brought to light. A woman's consciousness develops on her own terms in relationship to her values as a woman. A woman naturally projects her animus upon a man and all too often fails to separate herself from her animus side which causes her to think that she must throw out the instinctive woman and to try to be like a man—to ape him. This danger is greater when the mother is negative. A woman needs to respect the feminine values which reflect how she values herself as a woman. Undervaluation of her feminine nature causes a woman to feel inferior and she then overvaluates the masculine. I knew a woman with feminine values and an independent mind who was in the top management of an international airline in New York. When she left to be married, her employers told her they were particularly sorry to see her go because she had never come to a meeting without bringing something that no man would ever have thought of. She had a balanced sense of her worth as a woman.

Once I was at a small meeting where only women were present. We were discussing whether a certain man was properly qualified for a job or not. Some women thought not. I was urging that he be given a chance. Probably I was not too objective and let my feelings run, as one of the women turned to me and said: "Why Mary, how like a *woman* you are talking!"

The University of California's third symposium, "Man and Civilization: The Preface to the Potential of Women," began with these words:

> Whatever problems one may wish to lay at the door of the twentieth century, the substantial emancipation of women that has taken place in these sixty-odd years is surely an example of significant human progress. In the past, women necessarily defined themselves by the relationship they established with men. There was surely some choice available to women in previous periods. They could choose to be complacent or shrewish, domineering or submissive, efficient or burdensome. But their choices were very limited, and they were always made in terms of the masculine figure in their lives. Today, a great number of women can, if they choose, define themselves as independent, self-determining individuals. They can become fully human, since self-definition is the capacity marking human beings off from the rest of the universe. (Farber and Wilson 1963, p. vii)

Woman's' relationship to herself and her self-definition is psychologically exceedingly complicated, and care must be taken not to apply masculine standards here. For a woman to define herself in relation to another human being may be an expression of her eros nature, as contrasted with the logos nature of man. If she is conscious of what she is doing, there may not be a lack in her personality at all, nor a failure of self-determining independence. We must not forget that for women relationship is all-important. Whether to people, to the world with its physical and/or spiritual objects, or to the inner life and her own center, relationship is the keystone of a woman's psychological life. Without a living relationship she does not live—somewhere inside. But woman's eros knows many forms of expression.

The secret is that she is not just the daughter, the mother, or the wife. If she does not identify wholly with any one role, but realizes that she is something more, a woman may choose her life freely and with consciousness. Then she will be independent and self-determining. Many women in their attempt to find themselves get stuck trying to live up to collective masculine (animus) expectations instead of exploring what suits each one of them. The American woman is particularly vulnerable to this double bind, so that while she is looking for her own form of expression, the animus may trick her into a collective role.

Once I met a group of female American economists in the home of the president of the Swiss National Women's Organization. I thought that they were all professional women. I had grown up in the dark ages of prewar America when a career was the accepted thing and few of my college classmates thought of marrying early—in fact we pitied our friends who had the misfortune to marry before the age of 25. I innocently asked one woman what her work was. She smiled at me much too sweetly and reprovingly, and replied, "You know, I am only a homemaker." Making a home is one of women's greatest gifts, but the way she said it was artificial and animus-y, apologetic and sad, for she was caught in the collective role of the homemaker—dreadful word— and was ashamed of it.

This problem of self-definition is not so simple. It goes back to a woman's inner psychology and her relation to the divergent currents and conflicts of her own feminine self. It is cultural as well as individual. Psychologically we usually formulate it in terms of the animus, which undoubtedly plays a role, but taking it a step further back we come to the mother and the mother image, to a woman's relationship to herself. In analysis I can see its implications and demands in all of the women with whom I work. We are constantly working to clarify this self-definition, though we call it consciousness.

It is not only the so-called homemaker who realizes this problem, but also many professional women. Virginia Woolf wrote about it in her book *A Room of One's Own*, and Joanna Field in another book called *A Life of One's Own*—but the book with the most beautiful insights is Anne Lindbergh's *A Gift from the Sea*.

A woman's attitude toward her own feminine psyche, first experienced through her mother, is the foundation of her psychological house. Everything else is built on it. Even the animus can show the mother's influence, and an awareness of this side of her shadow is one of the best safeguards a woman can have against a devouring animus.

The first psychological stage in a woman's life is identification with her mother. It is through this mysterious process of identification that she learns what a woman is and how to be one. The chances are that as she was treated, so will she behave for good or bad, and so will she treat others. This, of course, is modified by her psychological structure and by her father. Behind the real mother looms the archetype of the great mother with the whole range of feminine nature from which to choose. What and how she chooses seems to-depend upon her mother relationship and her psychic constitution. The tremendous and fateful power that the mother seems to wield is not due to the human mother—though its victim always passionately believes this to be the case—but to what the mother has awakened in the unconscious of the daughter, which then proceeds to lead a secret life within her. The daughter absorbs like a sponge from the mother in accordance with her own nature.

In order that a woman grow up properly, incorporating and integrating in herself her psychological mother and daughter, she has to come to terms with some of her personal inheritance from her mother and determine whether or not it fits her nature. She has to look at what she has unconsciously absorbed and differentiate it, asking herself why she chose what she did.

The mother is basic in determining the daughter's fundamental attitude toward life. A positive mother image and a good instinctive connection—other things being equal—can give her a belief in life and a will to live. She is thus equipped with an attitude that trusts life, even though it may be wary. On the other hand, the daughter of the negative mother is often lamed by fear of life, a fear of death, and a fear of risking; her instincts are crippled and she is at a loss to know where to risk. Too often when she does risk it turns out badly, because something stands between such women and their own natures. For when a woman feels negative and rejects her mother, she becomes in her own eyes the rejected child. She then in turn rejects herself as a woman—on some level. One of the first things this rejection seems to affect is her own body and her feminine instinct; then the animus comes in to take their place. Observing such women, one can easily see this by the way they handle their bodies, by the way they move, walk, and sit. There is something unnatural about it for a woman. There are women who hate their female bodies, and often try to ignore, deny, or abuse their bodies. Instinctive disturbances and illnesses grow from such roots.

For example, frigidity is often conditioned by a woman's relation to her body and to her mother. Rejection of the woman within herself can cause a woman to be cold and unresponsive to a man. She has rejected the part of herself that responds. Or she may handle her sexuality like her image of a man, cutting it off from her feelings and becoming promiscuous. I have seen many daughters troubled by their sexual responses because they could not swallow what they considered their mother's immoral way of life. Not being able to identify with her mother on this score, the daughter unconsciously rejects her own sexuality, and becomes blocked and frigid.

Many women who want children do not conceive. Jung once commented that to have a child is an attitude of mind. Where this is a psychological problem, it is safe to say that it is connected to the mother relationship. On the other hand, women who have children easily, who are not frigid, yet who feel themselves to be negative mothers emotionally are therefore burdened with guilt. Having no proper pattern to guide them, they handle their children wrongly. They either neglect their children or overcompensate by being too "good" a mother, knowing in their secret hearts that they are "bad." A negative mother complex lies within such women.

A mother often passes on to her daughter the burden of her unlived and unconscious life. The dutiful daughter accepts her dear mother's burden, which is given her through the magic channel of *participation mystique*. This may be positive but more often it is not, and the mother passes on her darkest shadow. These are the children who do the exact and shocking opposite of what the mother hopes and wants. They are promiscuous, immoral daughters of upright, moral mothers. Such a heritage, positive or negative, grossly distorts the life of the daughter.

As I observe people's lives, I am more and more impressed at the way the relationship to the parents forms patterns which determine the fate of a child. The pattern of relationship to the mother (or father) sets up in the unconscious of the daughter certain expectations that she will be treated by life as mother treated her. It is sad and amazing to see how a woman can maneuver herself into situations where this expectation is fulfilled at all cost, many times against her better judgment. If she was rejected by her mother, or if she rejected her mother, she knows and sees to it that she will be rejected. These conditioned reflexes ingrained in childhood have appallingly long arms and influence many more of our decisions and actions, perhaps even our fate, than we are often aware of.

In analysis we have to go very deep to reach the level where this expectation can be found, confronted, and changed. To deal with the maternal heritage demands a ruthless honesty in facing the shadow, for such a mother can pass on a nasty shadow. Also the daughter must be willing to sacrifice a cherished immaturity, to give up the masochistic pleasure of being the victim of life as she was mother's victim, in other words, to stop being the daughter psychologically. When she realizes that the forces within her are creating her fate, she can begin to take over responsibility for her own unconscious. This means to stop blaming mother, father, husband, or children for her suffering and for cruel fate. As I have said, the goal of biological maturity is for the daughter to become the mother and have her own children. That she accept responsibility for her own unconscious is the goal of psychic maturity.

At this point, a woman has found the mother and daughter within herself. Until now, her life has been a search to bring the lost pieces together. The myth of Demeter and Kore (Persephone) underlies this particular drama of women: the mother looking for the daughter lost in the underworld and finding her again. It is also the night sea journey of women leading to the unity of their feminine psyche. Jung says in *Essays on a Science of Mythology,*

> Demeter and Kore, mother and daughter, extend the feminine
> consciousness both upward and downward. They add a
> "younger and older," a "stronger and weaker," dimension to it
> and widen out the narrowly limited conscious mind bound in
> space and time, giving intimations of a greater and more
> comprehensive personality which has a share in the eternal
> course of things. . . . We could therefore say that every mother
> contains her daughter in herself, and every daughter her
> mother, and that every woman extends backward into her
> mother and forward into her daughter. (Jung 1949, p. 225)

Women's mysteries in Greece dealt with this. The Thesmophoria at
the time of the sowing and particularly the mysteries at Eleusis, which
were basically of a transformative character, were important for a
woman's understanding of herself.

Neumann, in *The Great Mother*, writes,

> The woman experiences herself first and foremost as a source of
> life. . . . She is bound up with the all-generating life principle,
> which is creative nature and culture-creating principle in one.
> The close connection between the mother and daughter, who
> form the nucleus of the female group, is reflected in the
> preservation of the "primordial relationship" between them.
> . . . In the unique relief of a feminine cult both enthroned
> goddesses appear as the twofold aspect of the mother–daughter
> unity. Their significance is clear. . . . by the abundance of
> familiar symbols that belong to this context: flower, fruit, egg,
> and vessel. The whole is permeated by the self-contained
> transformative unity of the mother and the daughter, Demeter
> and Kore. This unity of Demeter and Kore is the central theme
> of the mysteries of Eleusis. . . . The one essential motive in the
> Eleusinian mysteries and hence in all matriarchal mysteries is
> the "Heuresis" of the daughter by the mother, the "finding
> again" of Kore by Demeter—the reunion of the mother and
> daughter. (Neumann 1955, p. 305–307)

No longer on a biological level, the union takes place on a different level.
For the transformation of the mother and daughter is a psychic reality,
and its fruit is the inner child.

To follow how these things unfold, form and transform, we begin
with the reaction of the daughter to her mother at birth. Does the baby
feel warm and protected, accepted and loved, and so sleep peacefully
and take the offered breast trustingly? There are babies who cry from the
moment of birth. The babies I know of who did this were not really

accepted or perhaps even wanted by their mothers. One mother said that her daughter started contradicting her in the womb. A baby seems to feel immediately how its mother feels about it. When the daughter senses that she is rejected by her mother, her feminine psyche reacts, causing a negative mother complex with all its consequences. When such a woman comes to analysis, the unconscious may be allowed to bring into balance the repressed contents and create a different and more positive attitude to her feminine nature.

Lucina

The story of a patient whom I will call Lucina gives us glimpses of how the mother and daughter come together to form the woman, and how the unconscious goes about mending this split. Lucina came into analysis at the age of 26 because of her fears. She was afraid at work. A dietician in a hospital, she was afraid of the doctors. She was afraid in every sphere of her life even though she was competent and gifted. Fear robbed her of all incentive, and she longed to lie in bed all day long and do nothing. She had a friend, Hans. As soon as she realized that she was in love with him she became afraid of losing him, and consequently grew doubly possessive. She suffered from depressions. Her grip on life was none too secure: she could well have walked in front of a car one day.

An attractive, tall, lean girl with lovely dark hair and eyes, Lucina was highly intelligent and honest. Psychologically she was introverted and intuitive. Her friend Hans was a law student working for his final exams. Although he came to see her regularly, he was unsure about whether he wanted to marry her. Her insecurity was increased by her animus, which was always trying to force him to make a commitment.

Lucina had reacted violently against her mother. Her parents had been divorced when she was three years old. They had planned to get a divorce several years before, but instead had had a baby, hoping to live happily ever after. So Lucina felt guilty for having failed in the task life had given her. Adding to this burden, her mother kept telling her that she should have been a boy, and that she had asked three times, "Are you sure that my baby is not a boy?" Consequently Lucina felt that she could never show herself as she was. Something else was expected of her and she had to play a role. Not being accepted by her mother as she was, she did not exist for herself, but led a phantom life. As a child she became ill when separated even for a night from her mother.

As a teenager she and her mother lived with her grandfather in Germany. One day during the war when she and her mother were crossing a large deserted square, her mother instantly disappeared as if whisked away by magic. At first it was a relief that her mother was not there; she made no effort to look for her. Then a second bomb struck and she realized what had happened: it was her first air raid. Her mother was not hurt; she had simply been lifted up by the vacuum. But it was a traumatic experience for Lucina because it acted out her unconscious wish to get rid of her mother. Somehow she had done this magical thing, so it alarmingly increased her fear and guilt. After this she became so nervous that she had to be sent to school in Switzerland.

At school she had a frightening dream in which she saw a large spider ascending the stairs to her room. With each step it grew bigger and bigger. She wanted to kill it, but though it moved slowly and deliberately, she was crippled and could not. Strangely, the next morning, in front of her door, in exactly the same spot, was a spider. This and the bomb "magic" are two interesting examples of synchronicity: the mother problem being constellated in her psyche, something happens in outer life. The bombing and the spider dream, although for years bygone, remained actual and full of power. Lucina experienced terror amounting to panic whenever she saw a spider. She was caught in the web of the negative mother, and in turn was busily spinning her own web. The spider is symbolically associated with the sympathetic nervous system, which reaches far down in reactions beyond our control. The spider symbolizes the mother and can represent the negative aspect of the unconscious mother image. The spider is closely connected to the witch. I mentioned to Lucina that the female spider eats the male, that it is a predatory, bloodsucking insect. It was as if she herself was sucking Hans in an effort to free herself by gaining power, and Lucina quickly understood this.

As always, the mother relationship played itself out in the little things of everyday life. She wondered whether she should write home every day, as her mother wanted her to, or only when she felt like it, which would be almost never. Should she send her laundry home? How often should she go home? Should she accept money from her mother? Her mother was constantly offering to pay for this or that. Lucina resented her mother's offer of the money as a kind of blackmail, as indeed it was.

Lucina swung between sacrificing herself too much and getting angry at herself for ignoring her own feelings. This conflict increased her resentment and resistance to her mother. She felt guilty when she did not go home, and hated herself when she did. With no standpoint of her own she fell victim to her mother's power game. She used the word "blackmail," but when I referred to her mother's power motives, she took exception to this, and was resentful—revealing her identification with her mother. This is typical of the negative mother complex, where the dependent daughter torn by love and/or hate is trying to escape to freedom. She must first disentangle herself from the identification. Suffering and struggling with these contradictory feelings is part of the process.

The more intense the daughter's feelings about her mother, negative or positive, the more closely bound she is to her. Hate is an active emotion that drives us to do something, while love lulls us into a comfortable unconsciousness. Fixation in one or the other is harmful when the time has come for growth and independence.

The baffling thing is that the daughter has learned through this identification with her mother what a woman is and how to behave. Often it seems to make no difference whether the learned pattern is for good and growth or for power and destruction. The old rule holds: as one is done unto, so one does unto others—unless one becomes conscious. Lucina railed against her mother for trying to hold her, devour her, enslave her. All the while she in turn was busily doing the same to Hans. Such women unconsciously go right on treating husband and children as they feel they were treated. This is the negative mother at work within the woman. Light must be thrown on the woman's own shadow if she does not wish to lead a meaningless and destructive feminine existence.

Such mothers use all kinds of tricks to hold onto their victims. Lucina's mother had no life of her own and she played the martyr—"life has treated me badly, poor me, who, of course, is in no way to blame—therefore everyone must be kind to me, to make up for my cruel fate, and particularly my daughter must." Lucina saw through this, but her own guilt, and the collective expectation that we ought to take care of the parents who have made so many sacrifices for us, bit deeply into her insecure soul.

These mothers consider their children part of themselves, because they once carried them within their bodies, and they can commit horrors of invasion upon another's personal rights and privacy. Sensitive children like Lucina suffer tortures with such an insensitive mother.

In therapy, we talked about how she and her mother were both playing the martyr and how such people characteristically try to maneuver themselves into situations where they will be hurt, forcing others to hurt them. Lucina saw that she should not play her mother's negative power-game of trying to get what she wanted by helpless suffering. Lucina commented that she had always felt that her mother was full of power, but until now she had never been able to see how it worked. We came to the conclusion that her mother was this way because she wanted love and was completely unconscious of her demands.

The daughter's answer to this was: "Yes, but I can do nothing about it. She freezes me. All I want to do is to run away and get as far away from her as I can. My mother keeps telling me I am brutal and feelingless, but I know that I am not really that way, but she makes me this way." When she told her mother that she wanted to be left alone for a while because she was working on her problems, her mother took the next train to Zürich, demanding to know what was wrong. It helped Lucina to begin to stand up for her own feelings when she understood that her reaction was a natural defense against such an unfeeling invasion of her personality.

The unconscious reacted with two dreams. The first:

> I was working in the hospital and a woman came in crying, "Come quick, there is a man down in the cellar who has a machine to make earthquakes! With the help of balloons, he can make them as strong as he wants." A great blast went off and the walls shook and cracked.

The day before the dream she had had a fight with Hans; he had not telephoned, and she had blown that up—like the balloons—into a bad quarrel. The man down in the cellar is the animus in the unconscious who is capable of shaking her very foundations if she lets him blow things out of proportion.

The next day she dreamed that she took the Number 15 streetcar to see Hans and was rammed through by the Number 7 streetcar which was the one her mother took to come and see her. The motorman in Number 7 was the dream man who made the earthquakes. Here again is the destructive animus from the mother, ramming into her feelings for Hans. She felt very threatened as her relationship to Hans was the one positive thing in her life.

In the second dream an aspect of her mother problem came up in her relation to her own body: she is nowhere in the dream. The woman who warns her in the first dream, described as being earthy, now is simply not there. In part it was her earthy shadow side that drew Hans to her. It was as if her intuition made her leap out of her body, as if a hole was left within her by having no real contact with her mother, who often represents for the daughter both the body and the earth principle.

An intense desire now rose within her to be rid of her mother. To reassure herself that her mother was taken care of she even put a marriage ad in the papers for her mother, compensating for the desire to destroy her.

Lucina began to fear her own magical thinking, as if thoughts could kill. She scarcely dared to act, for action would awaken the witch, and then she might really become the witch. When the destructive side is released, people become afraid of themselves, for a spark can start a fire. There was the danger that if she could not stand the rebellion against her mother and to look at her own shadow problem, her aggression could turn against herself, perhaps in the form of suicide.

In "animus women" whose feelings have been destroyed, relationships are often pictured as machines or prehistoric animals, and she had had two such machines in her dreams. Her relationship to Hans became of vital importance because he was the counterbalance to this negative side in her life. Hence she gave no thought at this time to dealing with her projections onto him; she could not have stood a reality-based relationship. Now he was her refuge and had to be safeguarded.

Lucina was at a point where the mother image had to be changed. Many daughters know derogatory things about their mothers which they cannot quite admit to knowing. They dare not give up their illusions of what a mother should be. It is part of the unifying process that when daughters give up the mother as an ideal image, they have to find that image in themselves. Her unconscious took care of it in a dream:

> *I am in my mother's house. I go to her room, but I cannot quite get the light to stay on. It keeps flickering on and off. I see my mother lying on her bed and realize that she is dead drunk. Then my mother staggers off the bed and falls to the floor. I beg her to talk to me, but she can't. I cry bitterly.*

When I asked her if she were finding out things about her mother which she had never recognized as true, she first denied it, and then confessed that that was the case, that her mother had made her a confidante some years before by telling her that she had had a lover for many years. She had even been tactless enough to tell Lucina that once Lucina had almost caught them in bed. Until this dream made her look at it, Lucina had repressed how she felt about this. The dream compensated for her too-high ideal of her mother by pulling her down. The flickering light points to her weak ego, her flickering consciousness. Being drunk one may be in the arms of Bacchus and lose sexual inhibitions. The mother's revelation of such an intimate affair shows how she regarded her daughter as part of herself. It was an invasion of the child's privacy as well as an unnecessary burden. Learning of her mother's conduct shocked Lucina's feelings more than her morals and she was able to withdraw her ideal projections. Consequently Lucina had a hard time expressing her feelings with Hans, and her erotic response was partially inhibited. The dream told her, too, that her mother cannot talk to her because contact and understanding is impossible, her mother being as she is. The object was for her to disentangle herself from her mother's shadow side by herself, and so to give up her mother. It became clear in the analysis that she was afraid of separating the mother archetype from her real mother because she might then lose her mother altogether, and therefore she had refused to look at the negative things.

After this her depression lessened noticeably, but now Lucina was putting the whole weight of giving meaning to her life on Hans and demanding more than he could give. Her aggressive animus was on the loose, and when a woman frightens a man's feeling side with her animus, the man retreats, leaving the woman alone and her feelings in the belly of the animus. Fortunately Hans exploded one night when she became too difficult. He told her that he was fed up, made love to her rather roughly, and then left. She was hurt and cried—like a little girl. Then it dawned on her that she had been playing a power game with him and was even grateful that he had reacted by putting her animus in its place.

Another heritage from her mother was the notion that all men are bad and will leave one sooner or later. To understand that there might be something between desertion and absolute unswerving faithfulness was beyond her. Many women project their own roving eye onto men and fantasize that they themselves are by nature towers of fidelity. Slowly Lucina could see that she was doing to Hans what her mother had done to her. She could also see that having made Hans her universe, she was presenting him with the bill. Women often find it hard to believe that when they give a man so much love, admiration, and devotion, when they sacrifice their lives, they are setting their own terms.

But she was beginning to value herself more and was looking for a new pattern for her feminine life. One night she dreamt:

> A very blond, made-up, hard-boiled woman, a typical vamp, drove a tiny car into a girl who was weak because she had had rickets as a child. I kept picking her up each time she was knocked down.

The night after she had this dream Lucina went out with Hans, dressed to play the vamp, which was her idea of how to hold a man. But after having made the effort, she was absolutely poisonous and made fun of him all evening. For of course she had no idea how to be the siren and was simply attempting to use her power under a different guise.

The night after this misdirected effort, she dreamt:

> *An old woman with a kindly face, full of human understand-ing, came to me, gave me some flowers, and said, "I am sorry but they are a bit faded, but perhaps you can make something of them anyway." I was happy to have them, and answered that all I needed to do was to put them into a pot with new earth, and they would bloom.*

These two dreams tell us the story of what is going on in her feminine development and how it works in the life situation. The weak girl who is knocked down by the vamp and has rickets because she never had enough sun and warmth is Lucina's weak feminine nature which never received enough love and care to grow properly. The hard-boiled woman is the collective idea of how to play a man's anima and so gain power over him. We often find such a reaction in women without differentiated feelings, who cannot relate personally. When this happens a role takes over which tries to knock down her growing side. But things change, and the little car is not nearly so dangerous as the street car, nor so collective. A feminine figure, however misguided, and not a diabolical motorman does the driving. Lucina's ego is now in the action, supporting the growing girl.

In the second dream there appears the archetype of the wise old woman; she understands human frailty and shows Lucina the means to her end. The flowers the old woman gives her are her feelings, which their names—forget-me-not, bleeding heart, etc.—show clearly. The night before with Hans, it had been *feeling* that she could not express. The wise old woman is exceedingly important, revealing her own basic feminine pattern so that Lucina can relinquish her personal mother. As in the mysteries of Eleusis, it is the flower that belongs to the daughter as a gift from the mother. The flowers are faded because she has not taken care of her feelings, and she realizes that her feelings—the flowers—need fresh earth, that is, she needs a new relationship to her instinctive side, to reality, to the earth mother.

We discussed this in the same hour, and in a nap after that hour Lucina had a dream.

> *Mrs. Briner is in my room talking to me. I am lying on my couch. I see she has only a head, and her body has disappeared. I wonder, "Why doesn't she realize that she has no body?"*

> *Then her face changes to that of a very old woman, all*
> *wrinkled up like a dried apple, but kind and full of wisdom.*
> *Finally I say, "but you have no body!" She answers, "Oh, that*
> *makes no difference, people like you often see me that way."*
> *This quiets me, and I see her body again. When Mrs. Briner*
> *gets up to go, I take a handful of pomme chips (potato chips)*
> *and stuff them into my mouth. I am shocked at my rudeness,*
> *first because I offered none to Mrs. Briner and second because*
> *I cannot say good-bye properly.*

This dream tells her—and me—that she does not see my body. I must give her more, because for her the body does not exist. That is precisely her problem, both as an intuitive person and as a woman. What we do not see in ourselves, we often cannot see in others. This body-earth-mother problem has been coming closer like the spider. Now it comes unmistakably into the analytical relationship. Up until this dream we had been relating through our heads as she had with everyone else. She was a thinking intuitive type and had to understand through her head, and I had probably been giving her too theoretical explanations. It was clear to me that she was projecting this problem, for I may not know I have a head, but I know I have a body. Her projection was mixed up with the archetype of the wise earth mother met in the flower dream. The apple face refers to the wisdom of life, of eating the apple of good and evil. Lucina described a peasant woman with a red handkerchief tied around her face, again making the connection with the soil, with the earth. The pomme chips, potato chips, also suggest this. Apple in French is called *pomme*, and potatoes are called the apples of the earth—*pommes de terre*. In Switzerland, potato chips are called pomme chips—or translated, apple chips. All Lucina had to eat was the fried or dried apples of the earth, the apple of good and evil. This probably means that she cannot yet stand to see the wise earth woman in herself—although that is what she is seeking.

In the mysteries of Eleusis, it is the daughter Kore who has the flower and the mother Demeter who has the fruit, pomegranate or corn. The *granate* is a fruit full of seeds, or potential, and *pom* is the old French word for apple. Here Lucina is trying to unite the daughter and mother in herself in order to make up her womanhood. She was given the flower in the other dream and now receives the fruit. Such fruit and flower symbolism runs all through her material. When I tell her in the dream that others who have this body problem see me with only a head and no body, she withdraws part of the projection and can see me whole. Her rudeness in the dream—she would never be rude in person—is an unconscious reproach to me for not giving her enough body: an invaluable hint to the analyst.

There followed a dream in which her grandmother, who died when she was 14, appeared to her asking,

> *"Why does no one give me any spring flowers?"*
>
> *"But grandmother,"* Lucina answered, *"How can I give you anything? You are dead."*
>
> *"Just so, no one thinks of giving anything to the dead."*

Here again the unconscious links her difficulty with feeling to both the archetype of the great mother and flowers. She took this dream to mean that she had not yet realized her feelings enough, indeed, that this side of her nature was still dead. Her own comment was that this dream brought home to her that she had not given enough trust and confidence to Hans.

A curious thing was that Lucina's love life had been more or less normal until she came to analysis; then she became frigid and had to make a whole new adjustment to Hans on the basis of her new knowledge of herself. She was discovering how inhibited and blocked she was and how cut off from her own feelings. She had also discovered that she was ashamed of her mother's erotic life. Her animus told her that sex is bad and immoral and that she should not be like her mother. Consciously she denied this, but it became a conflict that was getting in the way of her natural, animal side, especially to the extent that she looked down on sex. Whether we like it or not, sex belongs to the body and has the smell of the animal. But it belongs to our totality, and when we look down upon it, we become distorted. A man cannot make love to a spirit, but this is what a woman with too much animus likes to believe—that she appeals to a man with her spiritual nature. This is not to say that there is no spirit in love; quite the contrary, but a woman's real eros spirituality gets twisted when the negative animus dominates the picture.

Naturally she had trouble keeping her real feelings for Hans alive and not being demanding in a power way. After these dreams, the negative side reasserted itself.

Lucina had a kitten whose pure play and boundless energy became for her an expression of the joy of being alive just for the sake of living, something quite new to her. She saw the kitten as feminine, reflecting woman's natural animal nature in the best sense. But the old and the new were at war within her, and long-repressed emotions erupted in an attempt to destroy her new efforts.

In a dream she took a long, sharp knife and, holding her kitten over the edge of her bed so that she could not see it, she cut off its head. She was under the influence of the animus, which gave her the knife to destroy the spontaneous, natural woman within her. The knife is a favorite weapon of the animus with its cutting destructive remarks and thoughts.

At this time Lucina became greatly concerned about the meaning of life. It was a deep religious problem for her. She felt that suffering was meaningful and creative—she had to seek on her own and within herself a natural instinctive belief in life which should come from the mother. But the animus was out to try to destroy this. In another dream an airplane was coming toward her, shooting knives at her kitten to kill it, while she tried to protect it. Ever since the bombing raid of her childhood, she had associated airplanes with her secret, guilty death-wish against her mother. This secret death-wish had never before been admitted. The destructive aggression had been turned against the kitten as herself. Once again the whole problem that had erupted at the beginning with the bombing had to be reexamined. Lucina recalled once more that she had found her mother, with her dirty, bloody face, so repulsive that she could hardly bear to touch her.

She was afraid, afraid of those knives. She was afraid of that dissecting, destroying intellect that allows nothing natural to live. She could at last see that it is natural for a child to feel hostility, and that a child's way of getting rid of anything is to say that it is dead. On the one hand, she hated her mother for thwarting her life, while on the other hand she was desperately afraid of losing her, the only security she knew. It was her lack of security that had caused her to repress her destructive desires against her mother, which then turned against her cat, that is, against her own animal life, her body. In the next dream she was trying to commit suicide, but only wanted to kill her body, not her head. Here we see the fear of her body. The black masked figure of the executioner, a nightmare from her childhood, reappeared. Dreams of homosexual relations with her sister and of her cat producing sticky bubbles—like soap bubbles—of semen ended this frightening series. A chain of negative psychotic experiences and dreams is linked to the mother—first the bombing, then the spider, the earthquake man who blows up her world and rams her feeling life, the killing of her cat, and the aggressive animus—all indicating a desire to destroy her feminine side because she is afraid of it.

Finally Lucina has come to that nameless fear that she announced in her first hour. But all the while the unconscious has been building up the other side with the flower and fruit dreams, first the old woman who gave her flowers to plant in new earth, then the apple-faced woman mixed up with the analyst who brings knowledge of good and evil and, closer to home, her own grandmother to whom she should give flowers, expressing feeling.

Yet her latest dreams frightened and disgusted her, they were difficult to swallow, but as they were no problem for me to accept, she could make a bridge to herself through me and come to some understanding of her conflict.

At this time, exactly nine months after the beginning of the analysis, Lucina had a dream that proved to be the turning point.

> *I had arranged to meet Mrs. Briner in my room at midnight. I was asleep and awoke when she came in. The window was open, the room was cold. I told Mrs. Briner to wrap herself in a fur robe. I got out of bed to close the window. When I turned around she had slipped into bed. Suddenly it was quite dark in the room, though not entirely. It was as if a small light or candle was burning. She took me in her arms as if I were a small child and was tender to me. Then it was completely dark in the room, and she stroked with both hands the sides of my body, gently and softly. It was as if she were bringing my body to life. It is inexpressible, but was full of wonder and well-being. She said, "This is good for you and is what you need." I was filled with thankfulness and happiness. It was as if a supernatural, healing force flowed into me. I felt protected and contained by it.*

Here it is, the experience itself, very real to her, which counts and transforms. Little interpretation was needed. Midnight is a turning point, the end of an old day, the beginning of the new, the hour of darkness, of secret intimacy, the hour when spirits released from darkness can walk the earth. Ghosts of the past can be redeemed. Many rites are held at midnight, for it is the hour of transformation. Here the rite is the unifying of the mother and daughter to make the woman. The archetype projected on the analyst is that of the life-giving mother. The dreamer becomes alive, growing from a child into a woman in the dream. The room was old because the window was open. The vessel of transformation, in this case her room, must be closed, and the cold air of the animus shut out. As in all women's rites, the man often forbidden on pain of death, cannot be present, for it is a strictly feminine matter.

In the first step, Lucina is held as if she were a child, which she actually still was emotionally. The changing light parallels the descent into the unconscious. At the beginning there is light, though the dreamer is asleep—in the conscious situation, she is unconscious. But the confrontation of her problem through analysis awakens her—the arrival of the analyst in her room. Then the light grows dim, ending in complete darkness. Both are in the unconscious for the purpose of transformation. Here healing takes place through touch, an archetypal experience familiar to us from the Bible. Jesus touched the eyes of the blind to make them see (Matthew 20:34, Mark 7:33). They begged Jesus to lay hands on her who was deaf and dumb. People who have the gift of physical healing do so with their hands.

The numinosity of the dream reveals its archetypal quality. Lucina was filled with wonder and well-being. Thankfulness and happiness arose within her. But more than that, a supernatural healing force flowed into Lucina, containing and protecting her. The unconscious as the matrix and the spring of life are familiar images in Jungian psychology. Through analysis she came in touch with this deeper side of her creative, feminine nature. It was natural that in this process the analyst was an instrument of the unconscious, an image upon which she could project until she found this in herself. In this dream she takes to herself what belongs to her. As in the other dream where the analyst appeared, the body is a problem. But here the body is much more than physical sensation, sexuality, or soma itself. It is the ground of her feminine functioning, her feminine consciousness, a new awareness of life of which she is a carrier: the real reunion of the mother and daughter takes place within her. After this dream none of the matters we have been talking about were problems any longer. The emphasis soon shifted to her religious inquiry, and the analysis came naturally to an end. She was no longer just a daughter. She had become a woman.

References

Farber, S. M. and Roger H. L. Wilson, eds. 1963. *The Potential of Woman*. Third Symposium on Man and Civilisation, University of California at San Francisco Medical Center, January 25, 26, and 27. New York: McGraw-Hill.

Jung, C. G. 1949. *Essays on a Science of Mythology: The Psychological Aspect of the Kore*. New York: Bolligen Series XXII, Pantheon Books.

Neumann, Erich. 1955. *The Great Mother, An Analysis of the Archetype*. New York: Bolligen Series XLVII, Pantheon Books.

CHAPTER EIGHT

The Myth of the Hero

John Silber

*Adapted from a lecture at the symposium
Texas Myths: The Personal and the Collective Mythology, presented by the Institute for the Humanities at Salado, October 27, 1984. Copyright © John Silber.*

About John Silber

John Silber is the seventh president of Boston University where he is also professor of philosophy and law. Silber, one of the best-known university presidents in America, is a national spokesman for higher education and a writer on a wide range of social, political, and cultural issues. He is an outspoken critic of the political mismanagement of public schools. In 1987 the city of Chelsea, Massachusetts, asked Boston University to manage its schools, and in June 1989 a legislative action to allow this was authorized.

President Silber graduated *summa cum laude* in 1947 from Trinity University in San Antonio, and earned the Ph.D. at Yale. He was professor of philosophy, and university professor of arts and letters at the University of Texas at Austin where he also served as Dean of the College of Arts and Sciences.

Silber was a Fulbright Fellow at the University of Bonn and a Guggenheim Fellow at King's College, London. He is a member of the International Council of Advisors at the Institute for the Humanities at Salado.

President Silber has published widely on education in national magazines, including such essays as "Poisoning the Wells of Academe," (*Encounter*, August 1974), "Paying the Bill for College," (*The Atlantic*, May 1975), "The Flight from Excellence," (*Harper's*, June 1977), and "The Tuition Dilemma," (*The Atlantic*, July 1978). His numerous publications in philosophy include "The Ethical Significance of Kant's *Religion*," "Kant at Auschwitz," "Being and Doing: A Study of Status Responsibility," and "Human Action and the Language of Volition." His works on foreign affairs and military policy include "The Kennedy Doctrine," (*Strategic Review*, Fall 1984) and "Presidential Handcuffs"

(*The New Republic*, February 18, 1985). He has lectured at both the Air Force Academy and West Point on the topic "The Ethics of the Sword."

His inauguration address as president of Boston University, "The Pollution of Time," attracted widespread attention. On July 4, 1976, at Faneuil Hall in Boston, he delivered the City of Boston Bicentennial Oration, "Democracy: Its Counterfeits and Its Promise."

In the fall of 1989, Harper and Row will publish *Straight Shooting*, a book by Dr. Silber on the problems facing America.

President Ronald Reagan appointed Dr. Silber to the National Bipartisan Commission on Central America led by Henry Kissinger, and Silber serves on the Defense Policy Advisory Board and the advisory board of Radio Marti.

Silber has been honored by several of foreign governments. The Federal Republic of Germany has decorated him with its Grand Cross and Star of the Order of Merit; the French Republic has made him a Commander of the Order of Arts and Letters; he has also received the Peace Medal of the State of Israel.

It is a great pleasure and honor to have this opportunity to return to Texas and to renew my contact with the myths and folkways that I grew up with. That they have had their influence on me, I have no doubt. Certainly it is one of the primary functions of myth to give meaning to the conditions under which a people lives and develops; and this can be clearly seen in the mythology of Texas. I will consider one or two examples later on.

But let me begin with some general reflections on the role of myth in Western culture. Professor Donald Sandner, in his paper on the myths and arts of the Balinese and the Navajo, delivered to the Institute for the Humanities at Salado on October 27, 1984, provides us with a look at two cultures whose relationship to myth is strikingly different from our own. The Balinese, as Professor Sandner describes them, conceive of themselves as an inseparable part of a circumscribed geography. They live in a kind of waking dream, inhabiting a land where directions, colors, times, and topography are full of significance; but a land where significance ends at the sea.

Professor Sandner goes on to suggest that we, too, live within myths, and he mentions historical progress and science as examples of contemporary myths. In a certain sense he is correct: neither history nor science results, properly speaking, in myth, but we often understand them as if they did; further, they contribute a perspective on the mythical which is not available to the Balinese or the Navajo.

We also live, I believe, under the myth of Democracy: the struggle of America, even today, is to define the Democratic Hero. This attempt precludes our living, as Professor Sandner tells us the Balinese do, in a half-conscious balance of cosmic, social, and psychological forces. Consciousness, of as high an order as possible, is our great experiment, one of the primary achievements of Western culture. It provides the context in which we consider what the myth of the hero means for us.

Compare, for instance, an American's geographic sense with that of the Balinese, who believe that every direction in which one might travel, or from which one might see something approaching, has a meaning. What is our sense of the axes of our wider world?

For much of our history, the West meant the frontier, and the frontier meant a certain kind of hero, the rugged individualist. Now the frontier has reached its limit; the Far West these days means California, the Los Angeles detective, the freeways, the bridges and the hills of San Francisco, the gay rights movement, the hippies. To a New Yorker, of course, the West is merely that part of the country that doesn't count (Lionel Trilling was to boast that he had never ventured east of the Housatonic or west of the Hudson). To a Texan, the East is what has been superseded. To a Bostonian, the West is the unimportant world that lies vaguely beyond Dedham.

One of the peculiarities of the Texas myth is that even to this day, it preserves much of the character of the frontier hero. Texans still talk and act, or are thought to do so, in ways from which lesser mortals would shrink. Try picturing the different impact the following speakers would have on the denizens of a bar in San Francisco and on those in a bar in Texas. A man walks in and says:

> Let all sons of men b'ar witness; an speshully let a cowerin' varmint, named Sam Enright, size me up an' shudder! I am the maker of deserts an' the wall-eyed harbinger of desolation! I'm kin to rattlesnakes on my mother's side; I'm king of all the eagles and full brother to the b'ars! I'm the bloo-eyed lynx of Whiskey Crossin', an' I weighs four thousand pounds! I'm a he-steamboat. I broke a fullgrown alligator across my knee, tore him asunder an' showered his shrinkin' fragments over a full section of land! I hugged a cinnamon b'ar to death and made a grizzly plead for mercy! Who'll come gouge with me? Who'll come bite with me? Who'll come put his knuckles in my back?
> (Lewis 1902, p. 273)

And it happens, of course, that Sam Enright is right there in the bar listening, and Sam replies:

> I am for you! I was sired by a yoke of cattle; suckled by a she-bear; crossed the ocean on a saw-log. I got three sets of teeth and gums for another set; got a double backbone and fourteen rows of teats. (Hill 1888, p. 78)

In San Francisco, tolerant as it may be, those who engaged in this verbal agon would be locked up. In Texas, we might consider them archaic, but at least we would recognize their hyperbole as characteristic of our mythic traditions.

So much for the American sense of the West. But we must consider another direction, one much more actively present in our consciousness. For us, to travel south means to encounter Mexico and Latin America, Indian cultures older than our own, that Spanish/Indian culture so different from ours. It means the mythical landscapes of Gabriel Marquez, *machismo* and *soledad, revolución* and *milagro* (wonder or miracle).

Our horizontal consciousness, then, is of a mixed culture in which traces of many other cultures are active. On the vertical axis, few of us still believe that there is a heaven above us, and a hell below. Our sense of up and down has fused with our sense of what is internal to us and what is external. Literally, up means skyscrapers, radio towers, and stacked airplane traffic; down means oil, coal, and the hot center of the earth. But our mythical sense of up has merged into a sense of outwardness. To go far up is to go outward, into the unexplored reaches of space, to leave behind the de-mythologized moon, which is no longer Ben Jonson's "Queen and huntress, chaste and fair," or "Goddess excellently bright," but rather a great dust-covered pebble where no wind will ever disturb the ribbed footprints of the astronauts (Herford and Simpson 1932, p. 161).

From outer space we expect, to judge from the popularity of certain movies, either the benevolent and lovable *E.T.*, or the protean and disgusting *Alien*. Clearly we project, like the old mapmakers who peopled unknown seas with imaginary monsters, our own inner space onto outer space, other space. And in our inner space we expect to find the clues we need to become complete, integrated individuals.

The very ease with which any of us could call these ideas to mind demonstrates what I have said about consciousness. As Saul Bellow's Mr. Sammler says, we know, and we know that we know (Bellow 1970, p. 313). We cannot simply walk around and believe, much as we may envy the Balinese or the Navajo for being able to do so. We do not live either in an age of faith or naively in a world of myth. And so, as our educational system has always insisted, we are much closer to the late fifth-century Greeks, for whom myth was not merely a matter of belief but rather something to be questioned, dramatized, examined, and consciously used. This was the attitude of even the earliest Greek thinkers who tried to replace myth with rational explanation. Things, they argued, occur the way they do, not because of the actions of gods and heroes, but because the world is water, earth, air, and fire.

Plato, of course, is perhaps the greatest user, as opposed to believer, in myth. In his hands—in the myth of the cave, for instance—a story whose origins are mythical or religious becomes a thoroughgoing allegory, designed to demonstrate a system of virtue and knowledge. In *The Republic*, in the myth of the bronze, the silver, and the gold persons, and in the myth of Er, Plato recognizes that reason must employ the irrational in order to induce men to live rationally, to lead virtuous and courageous lives.

Along with Plato, the great Greek dramatists consciously used myth to explore and define their world. Sophocles's *Oedipus Rex* turns on one man's search for self-knowledge; this knowledge is of both something he has *done* and something which, whatever his will in the matter may have been, he *is*. Aeschylus's *Oresteia* discovers a balance between the avenging underworld Furies and the Olympian gods of justice, light, and reason who make up the Pan-Athenaic procession. Again and again we find the Greek dramatists balancing one myth against another; an investigation of single myths produces two or three interpretations and often, though not always, a reconciliation of different myths. All these occur not only on the mythical, but also on the conscious level. We do not learn, in the *Oedipus at Colonus,* whether Oedipus returns to the sky or to the earth, but we have a deep sense of what that question involves and of the relationship between the death of Oedipus, the hero Theseus, and the city of Athens.

This self-consciousness about myth is one aspect of the myth of the hero which I wish to raise today. The other, also bequeathed to us by the Greeks, is the relationship between democracy and heroism. What does the hero, the extraordinary man, have to do with the *demos*, the people in all their varieties of ordinariness? What effect *does* the hero have on the *demos*, what effect *ought* he have? Or is the concept of a democratic hero at best a paradox, at worst an oxymoron?

The Greek tragedians were preoccupied with just such questions. The essential tension in all the great plays is between the hero and the chorus, the chorus being the *demos*. In Sophocles's plays, the chorus has the last word, but it is the hero who has the highest levels of experience.

The chorus is often frightened, confused, or revolted by the heroic action of the play. The hero may turn to them for advice or comfort, or he may chastise them, scorn them, or simply move beyond them. In the end, the hero suffers violence, death, or translation to another world, and the chorus survives.

Shakespeare's *Coriolanus* dramatizes this tension between hero and people. Coriolanus, a general of heroic proportions, is forced to submit to the approval of the Roman mob in order to be elected to office. The electoral process involves his standing in the marketplace, showing his war wounds to the public and begging for their vote. He finds the event revolting and disgusting. The mob admires his heroic qualities (after all, he has saved them from their enemies both recently and on prior occasions—he is, in fact, so feared by the enemy that he is taken to be personally responsible for such peace as the city enjoys), but the mob also hates and fears his contempt. In other words, the *demos* is deeply ambivalent in its attitude toward the hero Coriolanus.

The Roman tribunes, on the other hand—envious, sly, and small men whose power would be checked if Coriolanus were elected—are violently jealous of him. He arouses in them *ressentiment* as Nietzsche and Scheler understood it, and they fear his *virtu*—just as lesser people always fear "the real thing." They know that if prompted, his arrogance and pride will cause him to turn on his fellow citizens. By controlling the mob, the tribunes bring about exactly the result they had hoped for. Coriolanus, infuriated by the people, speaks truthfully and outrageously and is finally banished from Rome. When informed of his banishment, he replies with an arrogance almost sublime in its magnificence:

> You, . . .
> . . . whose loves I prize
> As the dead carcasses of unburied men
> That do corrupt my air, *I* banish *you!*
> And here remain with your uncertainty!
> Let every feeble rumor shake your hearts!
> Your enemies, with nodding of their plumes,
> Fan you into despair! Have the power still
> To banish your defenders; till at length
> Your ignorance, which finds not till it feels,
> . . . deliver you as most
> Abated captives to some nation
> That won you without blows! Despising,
> For you, the city, thus I turn my back.
> There is a world elsewhere. (*Coriolanus*, III, iii, 120–135)

This completes the first great action of Shakespeare's tragedy. But the play goes further: in a sense, once banished from Rome, for

Coriolanus there is no "world elsewhere." His reputation as a great general and his status as a man without a city combine with his own wilfulness to further darken the tale. Once banished from Rome, Coriolanus becomes Rome's greatest enemy. He joins forces with the General Aufidius, once his greatest rival, Rome's most powerful enemy, and still the second greatest general in the world. Together they lead a huge force within sight of the walls of Rome. Coriolanus's heroism and pride have led to betrayal of the city which had fostered precisely these qualities. Drawing on the greatness that made him the noblest Roman he becomes the most treacherous. "A man outside his city," Aristotle observes, "is either a beast or a god" (*Politics*, I, ii). Coriolanus, godlike in his power and sense of his own nobility, becomes bestial in pushing those qualities beyond tolerable human limits.

But there is a final development in the play, which unifies what has gone before. The Romans send Coriolanus's mother to plead with him not to destroy Rome. The mother says much and Coriolanus says very little, but he agrees to spare the city even though he realizes that this will cost him his life.

Not only in *Coriolanus* but in many of Shakespeare's dramas, as in life, there is a point of no return. Until Duncan, for instance, has been murdered, Macbeth might still have been a "royal" man. By joining with Rome's enemies, Coriolanus passes the point of no return. He commits moral suicide. His virtues, everything that once made him great, are Roman virtues. In turning against Rome, he is destroying the city that has been his spiritual mother. When his natural mother speaks to him as Rome, his civic mother, he regains his integrity, but pays with his life. Morally saved but physically lost, the hero-become-villain is hero once more. His civic crime aborted, he is guilty only of betraying the alien Aufidius, who sets upon his old rival with a large number of men and kills him, trampling him into the ground. Thus the hero is again united with his spiritual motherland—Rome.

In following the movement of a great man from popular hero to villain and back again to a lonelier but perhaps even greater hero, Shakespeare explores the paradoxical status of the democratic hero. The proud, capable man must be both better than the mob and acceptable to the mob if he is to lead them and save them. The outstanding man must transcend and yet be accessible to the ordinary citizens of Rome. The difficulties of this concept must be examined if the democratic hero is to be understood.

In a democracy, a fundamental obstacle to the emergence of political heroes is found in the electoral process itself. If the people are to be led by heroes, the people will have to elect them. Every successful American politician knows that foremost among his tasks is the pleasing of a majority of his constituents. But what attracts everyone or even a majority? Goethe provides one answer:

> *Das Gemeine lockt jeden: siehst du in Kürze von vielen Etwas geschehen, sogleich denke nur: dies ist gemein.*
>
> (Baseness attracts everyone; if you see something being done quickly by a number of people, you may at once conclude that it is something base. Venetian Epigrams, Luke, ed., p. 119.)

Or, as William Blake put it:

> Great things are done when Men & Mountains meet.
> This is not done by Jostling in the Street.
> (*Manuscript Notebook 1808–1811*, Keynes, ed., p. 550)

Such problems may explain the sneering tone of some remarks recorded in Alexis de Tocqueville's diary in 1831:

> When the right of suffrage is universal, and when the deputies are paid by the state, it is singular how low and how far wrong the people can go. (Pierson 1938, p. 608)

Several days later, traveling on a steamboat, Tocqueville met a man who had left his first wife, gone to live among the Indians, taken an Indian wife, and also on many occasions taken to drink. On hearing that this man was also a former government official, who, like Huck Finn, had lit out for the territory, Tocqueville believed he had found proof that the people can go low and far wrong indeed:

> We are traveling at this moment with an individual named Mr. Houston [Tocqueville writes] . . . . This man was once Governor of Tennessee . . . . I asked what could have recommended him to the choice of the people. His having come from the people, they told me, and risen "by his own exertions." . . . They assured me that in the new western states the people generally made very poor selections. Full of pride and ignorance, the electors want to be represented by people of their own kind. . . . [To get elected,] You have to haunt the taverns and dispute with the populace. (Ibid., p. 607)

But Tocqueville was soon forced to reappraise the wisdom of the backwoods Jacksonians who had elected Sam Houston governor of Tennessee and would, a few years later, elect him the first president of the Republic of Texas. Fascinated by this man of the people, Tocqueville questioned Houston about his life among the Indians and before long was taking notes on their religion, their government, their concepts of justice, and the roles of their women.

> Does it seem to you, [Tocqueville asked,] that the Indians have great natural intelligence?
> Yes [Houston replied,] I don't believe they yield to any human race on this point. However, I am also of the opinion that it would be the same for the negros. (Ibid., p. 613)

The conversation then turned to an analysis of U.S. government policy towards the Indians, and once again Tocqueville took copious notes. Both men, it turned out, were concerned with preserving the Indians. Summing up his impression of Sam Houston, Tocqueville no longer sneers, but is sympathetic and, finally, deeply impressed by this man of the people:

> The disappointments and labors of all kinds that have accompanied his existence have as yet left only a light trace on his features. Everything in his person [concludes Tocqueville] indicates physical and moral energy. (Ibid., p. 611)

Sam Houston is one type of the democratic hero: ambitious, large-spirited, driven by a personal code of honor, in touch with the people and with the land, a friend to the indigenous peoples and yet one of the foremost in promoting the spread of civilization into their territories. As Antony says of Brutus in Shakespeare's *Julius Caesar*,

> His life was gentle [i.e., noble], and the
>   elements
> So mix'd in him that Nature might stand up
> And say to all the world "This was a man!"
> (*Julius Caesar*, V, v, 74–76)

But it is surely worth remembering that Houston, honored as a genuine hero, died an outcast, despised by his fellow Texans for opposing Texas's secession from the Union. Houston and other heroes have found that doing the right thing is seldom popular and often fails to achieve success in any obvious sense. Indeed, recognizing this fact—

braving the unpopularity of opposing the popular—is one of the traits that defines the hero, especially in a democracy.

In September, 1960, Dr. Frances Oldham Kelsey, an official of the Food and Drug Administration responsible for the approval of new drugs, received an application for a new sedative called thalidomide. Although the manufacturer pressed again and again for quick approval, Dr. Kelsey withheld it because she found the testing incomplete. This led to accusations that she had libeled the manufacturer. After pressuring Dr. Kelsey for a year, the manufacturer conceded that the drug had been withdrawn from sale in West Germany. Incredibly, however, he continued to press the application in the United States. Dr. Kelsey held firm. By March, 1962, the association of thalidomide with birth abnormalities was clear, and the manufacturer finally withdrew the application. As a result of Dr. Kelsey's heroism, this country was spared the birth of perhaps thousands of seriously deformed infants. Europe, lacking similar heroes in its bureaucracies, was not spared.

Let us ask another question raised by *Coriolanus* about the democratic hero. Besides the relationship of the great man, with his higher level of consciousness, to the crowd, with all its vagaries and vulgarities, we might ask about the peculiar role of the military hero, or more generally, the man of force. Two of the greatest speeches produced by democracies are eulogies for those who died in battle: Pericles's funeral oration and Lincoln's Gettysburg address. And these great orators use a similar argument: that the deeds of dead soldiers are difficult or perhaps impossible to celebrate or memorialize in words. Speaking of the Gettysburg battlefield, Lincoln said, "The brave men, living and dead, who struggled here, have consecrated it far beyond our poor power to add or detract." And 2,000 years earlier Pericles, defining what makes a democracy great, observed:

> To me, . . . it would have seemed sufficient, when men have proved themselves brave by valiant acts, by acts only to make manifest the honors we render them. . . . For it is a hard matter to speak in just measure on an occasion [such as this]. (*History of the Peloponnesian Wars*, II, xxxv)

Yet Pericles also emphasizes that the essence of democracy is peaceful interaction between man and man. And Thucydides, who reports Pericles's speech, ascribes much of the later tragedy of the Athenian empire to an overemphasis on military adventurism.

The question may be posed in this way: What is the relationship between the peaceful working of a democracy and the man of force? Our own American military heroes have given us presidents that are great, good, and deficient: Andrew Jackson, Dwight Eisenhower, and Ulysses Grant.

Still another question raised by *Coriolanus* involves what might be called the shadow of the hero, that is, the shadow cast by the hero—his effects on other men. On the one hand, he exalts and motivates; on the other, he intimidates and demeans. This tension, particularly severe in a democracy, is recognized in Pericles's funeral oration. Having spoken of honor, he directly addresses the relatives of those who died defending Athens:

> But for those of you here who are sons and brothers of these men, I see a great conflict awaiting you. For the dead are always praised; and you, even were you to attain to surpassing virtues, will have a hard time being thought of—not as their equals, but even as men slightly inferior. (Ibid., II, xlv)

Under the rubric of the heroic shadow, I group several negative effects of greatness. Among these are, above all, resentment—the envy and rancor greatness evokes among the less great; irresponsibility, as ordinary men look to the great to shoulder all burdens; discouragement for future generations; and by no means least of all, harm—since greatness may consist in doing great evil. But perhaps the most far-reaching effect of the hero's shadow is what we may term the antihero. Not the villain, not the greatly evil man, but precisely the *anti*hero. He is a strange being perhaps, but we have all seen him.

The examination of the hero and the ordinary man, the man of force and the peaceful citizen, and the shadow of the hero are aspects of our central problem. All concern the relationship between the hero and the people for whom he is a hero, and each will add to our comprehension of the democratic hero.

Now consider our first question. What can, what should be the relationship between the hero and a democratic people? The answer is that democracies, like all human societies, and indeed like all individuals, need heroes and require a vision of greatness if they are to achieve their potential. The Athenian poet Aristophanes has his chorus praise Athena, the presiding goddess of that democratic city-state: "Thou great aristocrat: make this people noble. Help us to excel" (*Thesmophoriazusae*, penultimate chorus). True excellence, the poet suggests, is accessible to all, not merely to those of noble lineage. It is essential to American democracy, no less than it was to Athenian democracy, to reconcile greatness of soul with liberty and equality.

Our backgrounds inevitably shape our ideas about how greatness and equality are to be reconciled. My own were molded by my Texas origins and by the role of the hero in Texas culture. Consider the fall of the Alamo, a story which is part history, part legend, and part myth. New light has been shed on it by the great actor, Peter Ustinov.

He was asked by a Texan how he had liked making *Viva Max,* a fantasy on the retaking of the Alamo by the Mexican army. First of all, Ustinov said, he had not been terribly popular walking the streets of San Antonio dressed as a Mexican general.

But he remembered, he said, a meeting with Governor Preston Smith of Texas. The governor ritually retold how the leader of the Texans, Colonel Travis, had drawn his sword, cut a line across the dirt floor, and voiced his famous challenge: "All who choose to fight and die for Texas's independence, cross over and stand with me."

"And Governor Smith concluded,"—and at that point Ustinov developed a rich Texas accent—" 'Every Texan crossed over that line with Colonel Travis.' " "But Governor," Ustinov replied, "if all those in the Alamo crossed the line and stayed, and if they all died with Colonel Travis, how is it that we know the story?"

The Governor was undaunted: "Mr. Ustinov, that's because a French feller named Rose refused to cross the line; he turned tail and ran. But he weren't no Texan."

"Ah," Ustinov responded. "Would he perhaps be the one who inspired that famous song 'The Yellow Rose of Texas?' "

While we might owe our account of the heroism of Davy Crockett, Jim Bowie, Colonel Travis, and the others to the Yellow Rose of Texas, this is highly unlikely. Rose would hardly have talked. Who then was the anonymous poet, the blind Texas Homer of the tale? Who composed this epic event, whose end no Texan ever witnessed? What other source could there be than the fact that the defenders, outnumbered some twenty to one, were prepared to give their lives for freedom—that they, like Patrick Henry, set a higher value on liberty than on life? The less poetic interpretation—that the defenders were just too stupid to leave—has limited appeal in those parts or in any others.

The story of the Alamo, as we now have it, provides a rational and satisfying account of an otherwise inexplicable event. The heroic myth reconciles the people to their past. It also provides us with democratic heroes who are satisfyingly manageable: heroism is more tolerable in the dead, since the dead no longer constitute a threat to the living.

But heroism has never been merely consigned to the graveyard or to public statues of our honored dead. Educational institutions—in all societies, from the simplest to our own—have considered courage as a virtue and the hero as exemplary, an ideal to be imitated. Education prepares individuals in a democratic society to embrace the hero. In recent years the encouragement of heroism—or any other moral quality for that matter—has been frowned on in some educational circles. But in Texas the sense of the heroic survives. Young people still learn of heroes and see them as models for emulation.

Not only in Texas but throughout the United States, education—which our democracy counts among the rights and duties of every citizen—ought to present the heroic as a model for each individual. The philosopher Alfred North Whitehead has argued that moral education depends upon our recognition of the essential role of heroes in our life: "The sense of greatness," he wrote, "is the groundwork of morals" (1949, p. 106). A surprising statement, for Whitehead is claiming that morality, which establishes the norms for action, is grounded in an appreciation of greatness, which, by transcending the norm, intensifies one's motivation to attain it. Whitehead continues:

> Moral education is a fundamental education of the whole self into action or being. This is impossible apart from the habitual vision of greatness. If we are not great, it does not matter what we do or what is the issue. (Ibid.)

And this sense of greatness, he held, must be embodied in myth or story, rather than in some catalogue of moral virtues or duties held up for us to strive toward. "The sense of greatness," he says, "is an immediate intuition and not the conclusion of an argument" (ibid., p. 105). The story of the brave defense of the Alamo is a more powerful image of moral greatness than any to be obtained by a course in ethical theory. An essential and traditional function of literature and art is to provide these immediate intuitions of greatness—hence the central role assigned to literature and art in liberal education.

Simply recall how liberal education has fulfilled this function in the past. Documents from the Boston school system a century ago make it clear that the inculcation of the heroic life was crucial to the curriculum: Macaulay's *Lays of Ancient Rome*, Milton's *Paradise Lost*, Scott's *Ivanhoe*, and *The Boys' Froissart* were studied in high school. In grammar school students would already have read about the history of England and the United States; such figures as Queen Elizabeth, Henry V, Sir Walter Raleigh, Washington, Lincoln, and Jefferson were held up to the young as models to be emulated. The circulating library for the grammar schools included *Ivanhoe*, Towle's *Magellan*, Longfellow's *Evangeline*, *What Mr. Darwin Saw in his Voyage Around the World in the Ship*

Beagle, versions of *Tom Brown* and *Robinson Crusoe,* and Gilman's *Magna Charta Stories.*

High school was, it seems, considered the proper time at which to introduce mythology; Berens's *Handbook of Mythology* was required reading. The school board stipulated that Cooper's *Deerslayer* and *Pathfinder,* Longfellow's *Hiawatha,* and Herodotus on the *Persian Wars* were to be available in at least 35 copies per class (*School Document Nos. 6–1884, 15–1884, and 11–1884*).

In *McGuffey's Readers,* the dominant textbooks of American education in the nineteenth century—they began to appear in the year Texas gained its independence—the emphasis is less dramatic but no less edifying. The heroic is domesticated and brought within the purview of a child: greatness becomes accessible. Examples of Roman generals, European kings, queens, and knights are therefore rare. The greatness is of a smaller scale, but its relevance has been widened, democratized. A prudent, honest, confident George Washington; a steadfast, compassionate Lincoln—these appear in the company of wise grandmothers, sacrificing parents, and good children. The moral impulse behind *McGuffey's Readers* is the same as that which produced a sign on the wall of the San Antonio YMCA in the 1930s. It said, "Don't wait to be a great man. Be a great boy!"

Unfortunately for us and for our age, our educational system has become less and less effective in transmitting our birthright of heroism, our patents of potential nobility. With the tragic disappearance of the idea that every educated person should read certain books (the Bible, the *Iliad,* the dialogues of Plato, to mention only three), we have lost that inspiriting greatness of which Whitehead speaks. I have made it a point, when welcoming freshmen to Boston University, to ask if anyone knew what a pair of classical heroes, Achilles and Patroclus, had in common with the biblical heroes Jonathan and David. One of the few students who had heard of any of them pointed out that they were all dead. Not one knew what the pairs of heroes had in common. In despair, I asked them, "Well, what do they have in common with Starsky and Hutch?" At last they knew what I was looking for. That the paradigm of male friendship for this generation of students is Starsky and Hutch measures the decline of our educational system and our culture. The students often asked, "What's better about these old versions of friendship? Why aren't Starksy and Hutch more relevant? And why isn't one myth of the hero as good as another?"

The falsity of the dogmatic assertion of moral and aesthetic equivalence is obvious to those who are truly literate. The Old Testament is a book not only sacred to three major religions, but a book that is a superb distillation of human experience, good and ill. It not only has heroes, it has a wide and coherent range of heroes. It is a continuing saga of heroism in a world created by a single supreme being.

And the heroes of the *Iliad* display the basic modalities of human existence: the importance of learning from life—of ripening, the meaning of excellence, the nature of friendship, the necessity of loyalty and courage, the tragic solitude of our condition, and the inevitability of death.

None of this is now a part of the common experience—the common curriculum—of high school graduates. This means that typical freshmen entering college lack the texts of their potential humanity, even their spiritual survival. They will all face, possibly before they graduate, surely before they are 30 or 40, the loss of close friends or a family member, the loss of love, disappointed hopes. Ignorant of the heroes of ancient Greece, ignorant of biblical heroes, ignorant of greatness, they will not know David's lament on the deaths of Saul and Jonathan. David mourned:

> The beauty of Israel is slain upon thy high
> places;
> how are the mighty fallen!
> From the blood of the slain, from the fat of
> the mighty, the bow of Jonathan turned not
> back, and the sword of Saul returned not
> empty.
> Saul and Jonathan were lovely and pleasant in
> their lives, and in their death they were
> not divided:
> they were swifter than eagles, they were
> stronger than lions.
> Ye daughters of Israel, weep over Saul, who
> clothed you in scarlet, with other
> delights, who put on ornaments of gold upon
> your apparel.
> How are the mighty fallen in the midst of the
> battle!
> O Jonathan, thou wast slain in thine high
> places.
> I am distressed for thee, my brother
> Jonathan: very pleasant hast thou been
> unto me; thy love to me was wonderful,
> passing the love of women.
> How are the mighty fallen, and the weapons of
> war perished!
> (2 Kings 1:18–27)

Had Achilles heard David's lament, he would surely have said, "These words would have graced the death of Patroclus." Achilles could not hear these words; we can. We can, but do not. Lacking these texts of greatness, we may then find ourselves dumb when we most need to articulate our grief, deprived of the company of those who have suffered greatly before us and like us.

So the answer to our first question about the nature of the democratic hero—the relation between the great and the ordinary—is that each individual must imitate the great. It might be objected that such imitation is incompatible with individualism. In refutation, Goethe again comes directly to my point:

> *Gleich sei keiner dem andern; doch gleich sei jeder dem Höchsten.*
>
> (Let none be like any other; but let each be like the Highest. *The Four Seasons,* Luke, ed., p. 130.)

Our second question concerns the relationship between the hero of force and those whom he protects or of whom he takes advantage. Consider the legendary lawmen of Texas, our Texas Rangers, who in their origins were quite different from what they are today. The myth is symbolized by the statue in the airport at Dallas which proclaims "One riot, one Ranger." Behind this is the reality which led to the myth. Because the Rangers are a part of recent history as well as myth, we can compare the two.

Perhaps at this point a clarification is necessary. We shall consider the origins of the Texas Rangers, whose conduct and practice in those early frontier days bear little relation to their activities after the frontier was settled. Nor do I intend to denigrate the accomplishments of the earlier Rangers, which were nothing less than the bringing of law and order into a region that was, without their presence, chaotic and violent. However, to examine the early Texas Rangers and the myth that grew up around them, we must see them as they were, both good and bad. Myth sometimes arises to ennoble the man of force whose actual deeds do not match the ideals and aspirations of his calling. I believe this is true of the Texas Rangers and can be acknowledged without either demeaning the Rangers or losing sight of their accomplishments.

I am here employing the word "myth" in the looser popular sense of something that ranges from illusion to falsehood. Elsewhere I have used the word "myth" in its more profound meaning.

The mythical Texas Rangers emerge in Walter Prescott Webb's book *The Texas Rangers: A Century of Frontier Defense*. It is a Ranger Captain who is reported by Webb as saying:

> No man in the wrong can stand up against a fellow that's in the right and keeps on a-comin'. (Webb 1935, p. 455)

And no book that begins by invoking the chauvinism of A. E. Trombly's poem on the Texas Rangers, which includes the peculiar notion that Mexicans, Apaches, and Comanches are all "strangers" to Texas, can be far from the mythical in that debased sense that reaches to falsehood. Trombly versifies:

> Ask the Apache the why of his going,
> Ask the Comanche, he's not without knowing;
> Question the Mexican thief and marauder
> Why his respect for the great Texas border;
> Question them all, these beaten-back
>   strangers,
> White-lipped they'll tremble and whisper "The
> Rangers!" (Ibid., p. 3)

But perhaps the best way of comparing fact and emerging myth is to focus on a specific incident, like the El Paso salt wars. There were two factions struggling for control of the Salt Lakes in El Paso; one was led by an Italian named Don Louis Cardis, the other by a certain Charles H. Howard. Cardis, a member of the legislature, had long been friendly with the Mexicans. He and his friends stood to lose should Howard have things his way. But let Webb tell the story:

> Cardis soon perceived that Howard was coming to the head of the party, and he began to steal away Howard's influence. Howard avenged himself by whipping Cardis publicly on two occasions. It was the brutal and direct American way set against the subtle cunning of a Mexicanized Italian. Back of Howard was the handful of Americans and a few Mexicans and back of Cardis was a horde, an ignorant rabble under the direction of a greedy priest. (Ibid., pp. 349–350)

Finally Howard, who was not only an entrepreneur and democrat, but more importantly, a judge—one who, like Roy Bean, set Texas standards for justice—grew impatient of the law's delays. One October afternoon he took his shotgun to Cardis's office. Cardis, rather than drawing on

Howard, stood behind a high desk which protected the upper part of his body; so Howard emptied one barrel of buckshot into Cardis's legs and, when he fell, emptied the other into his heart.

The "ignorant rabble" (as Webb described the Mexicans) were enraged. Subsequent events convinced them that Howard would never be brought to justice (ibid., pp. 353–355).

Then Webb, under the heading "Death to the Gringos," records what he considers a series of heroic deaths (ibid., p. 360). But for a truer account of these subsequent events, the reader will do well to turn to the documentary and eyewitness evidence collected by Webb's student, Mr. C. B. Smith (1928, pp. 73–77).

Smith tells how 20 Rangers were called in to protect Howard. Once the Rangers had arrived, Judge Howard's next move was to go through town daring the Mexicans to kill him and shouting the time-honored insults: spic, greaser, and so on.

That night Mexicans of sufficient arms and number surrounded the house where Howard and his Ranger peace force of 20 men were staying. After four days, during which two Rangers were picked off, the two sides agreed to talk. While the talks were underway, despite his bodyguard of two, Howard was seized by the Mexicans and executed; soon after, so were his bodyguards. The rest of the force surrendered and gave up their weapons. Thanks to the intervention of a Mexican priest, the one whom Webb described as the "greedy" leader of an "ignorant rabble," they were saved from massacre.

Finally, to cap our comparison, consider Webb's summation of the character of a Ranger captain of those days to the conduct of the Rangers sent to protect Howard:

> The main requisite of the Ranger captain is intelligence. He is all mind, and his mind works, not only in emergencies, but ahead of them; he anticipates the contingency and prepares for it. As part of this intelligence he must have judgment, and it must be almost unerring. A Ranger captain, to be successful, must combine boldness with judgment. (Webb 1935, pp. 79–80)

Or, as Webb puts it more succinctly, "The mind of the great officer encompasses that of the outlaw" (ibid., p. 391). Of the Texas Rangers and Howard, he might have said that the *actions* of a great officer also encompass the *actions* of a great outlaw.

For one final insight into the actual life and mind of the Texas Rangers of that period, in contrast to Webb's mythological report, consider two quotations from Ranger Ira Aten, in charge of patrolling fences in West Texas. The first demonstrates the depths of his diplomacy and personal resource, as he says:

> Nothing will do any good here but a first class killing and I am
> the little boy that will give it to them if they don't let the fence
> alone. (Ibid., p. 423)

The second quotation from Aten reveals a rarely stressed aspect of the Ranger's function as double agent or double-crosser. Apparently the actions of the Rangers bore some resemblance to the recently discovered and politically more controversial handbook published by the CIA. The quotation shows Ira as something like a weary spy from one of John le Carré's novels, ready to "come in from the cold":

> These are my last fence cutters whether I catch them or not. . . .
> We have had to tell ten thousand lies and I know we won't get
> away without telling a million. (Ibid., p. 423)

True stories of the Texas Rangers might persuade us of the truth of something which the novelist James Jones once said: "The world will not be civilized until the last brave man is dead." This, of course, is a mistake, but we are tempted to make it. It is a natural reaction to the example of deficient heroes. But we must not allow the deficiency of heroes to obscure their real accomplishments. The Texas Rangers and other lawmen who brought peace and the rule of law out of unrest and the rule of the strongest were heroes, however flawed.

To conclude then: the uncritical idealization of the hero of force produces a false version of reality, which denies all claims and perhaps even the humanity of the victims. It holds up the mirror not to nature, but to the narcissistic ego.

Now to our third problem—the shadow cast by the hero. I have divided this into a number of aspects, the first of which is the malicious envy aroused by the very existence of greatness. Many heroic myths and legends take account of this *ressentiment* by creating particular gods or men who express this dark shadow effect of heroism.

In the Norse myths, the wisdom of Odin, the giant-killing power of Thor, and the beauty of Idun are constantly threatened by the deviousness, envy, and malice of the god Loki. Homeric gods provide no single analogue to Loki, and the reason is surely that they are less heroic. The envy and destructiveness focused in the figure of Loki are diffused throughout the Homeric pantheon.

All attempts of the Norse gods to banish, bully, or imprison Loki are destined to fail. He is a consummate shape-changer, a completely unscrupulous liar who, like all such creatures down to the Frog Prince, has a way with women. On Ragnarok, the Day of Doom, Loki will, out of sheer malice, join with the frost giants, the fire giants, the great serpent, and the great wolf to destroy heaven and earth. For Loki the sense of greatness is not the foundation of morals, but a gradual evolution from moral indifference to evil on a grand scale—that is to say, to cosmic wickedness.

A more contemporary example of a man overshadowed by the hero, and acting from envy and malice, is Lee Harvey Oswald, the assassin of President Kennedy. Here, indeed, one of the Norse myths illuminates that terrible event. The myth in question tells of the death of the god Balder, most beautiful and gentle of Norse gods.

Loki, living in the shadow of stronger, wiser and more splendid beings, hated Balder. Loki's threats frightened Frigg, Balder's mother, and she journeyed through the entire world, asking and receiving from every being she addressed, a promise to help and never to harm Balder.

As Frigg was returning home she noticed mistletoe growing on an oak. She secured the oak's promise, and she started to ask the mistletoe, but thought, "It's too small and soft to do harm." She entered Valhalla and told her son that all was well.

After Frigg's return, the gods played at throwing spears, darts, swords and axes at Balder. Only Hoder, Balder's blind brother, could not participate. All the others watched with amusement and wonder as their weapons veered and fell harmlessly at the feet of the laughing god.

A disguised Loki drew the whole story, including her oversight, out of Frigg. He then went to Hoder, handed him a dart made of mistletoe, and guided him to the right position. Hoder, glad to be able to join in the game, threw. The dart failed to veer, and Balder fell dead.

Examine briefly, in terms of the myth of Balder, the events of 1963 in Dallas.

The dart was passed to Hoder, Balder's blind brother. It is not perhaps too fanciful for us to recognize in Oswald a modern counterpart of the hero's blind brother, who, because of his blindness could kill with some degree of inadvertence. Certainly like Loki, or like Cain, Oswald killed out of resentment and outrage. But in certain crucial respects he is no more than a blind Hoder, who kills because a weapon is handed to him. It is handed to him by a culture that tends to view violence, as the Norse gods viewed sport that promised to be harmless, as nothing more than a game. But the weapon may also have been handed to him by a force in which the envy and malice of Loki are embodied. Like Hoder, Oswald may have been a tool of a far greater force: in this case, the Soviet/Cuban connection. But he was also, we may suggest, moved like Loki by envy and hatred of what is splendid and successful.

It is even more interesting to note that Oswald viewed himself as a kind of hero. And some American myths encouraged this. I think of the (perhaps mythical) attribution to John Wilkes Booth of the phrase, after his assassination of Lincoln, *"Sic semper tyrannis."* Oswald almost certainly had never heard of Loki, but he certainly knew of John Wilkes Booth, the Lone Ranger, and Superman. These popular mythical figures declare that to the individual everything is possible. Superman decides whether or not a certain person dies, or whether the whole world survives. The Protestant ethos, with its emphasis on the individual, has done much to encourage this myth, and parables of Jesus and the Sermon on the Mount are often misread accordingly. It leads to, and today is inseparable from, a romantic exaltation of the individual combined with denigration of all institutions and ignorant and dangerous underestimation of their importance.

But whatever the trappings, the experience communicated is that volitional power alone can transcend the framework on which it depends. The contrary idea, volitional responsibility directed from within a social structure, based on the inescapable status of all individuals—in other words, the foundation out of which responsibility can emerge—is missing from these myths. In them the hero is ultimately self-grounding. Whatever good or evil he may attempt proceeds from nothing but his own volition.

Out of this perspective a blind child like Oswald, or any of today's terrorists, may think of himself as a Lone Ranger, as a Messiah, as the man who by his own individual decision can transform history and bring about victory for whatever he conceives to be good. These delusions, too, are a part of the shadow of the hero.

But besides the villain, the man of evil whether great or small, there is another being who lives in the shadow of true heroism: the antihero. By the term "antihero" I do not refer to those who are motivated by resentment or envy in response to the hero. Neither Loki nor Lee Harvey Oswald, nor Tamburlaine nor Milton's Satan, are antiheroes. They are perverse heroes, evil heroes. However wrongly, however terribly, they *act.*

The same is true of Lady Macbeth and of Richard III, who share a ferocious and devious energy that has its own kind of magnificence. When Richard III announces that:

> Since I cannot prove a lover
> . . .
> I am determined to prove a villain;
> (*Richard III*, I, i, 28–30)

Or when Lady Macbeth, to further her husband's ambition and her own, says:

> . . . Come, you spirits
> That tend on mortal thoughts, unsex me here,
> And fill me from the crown to the toe top-full
> Of direst cruelty! Make thick my blood
> Stop up the access and passage to remorse.
> (*Macbeth*, I, v, 41–45)

—we are in the presence of vicious, but not unheroic persons.

Nor by "antihero" do I mean Hitler or those coming from outside a given culture who wage war against it.

Nor do I mean those who, from within a culture, achieve an understanding or an approach to life which challenges what the culture considers heroic: Job, for instance, refusing to accept the arguments of his comforters; or Hamlet, a man whose intelligence and excessive self-consciousness render him unable to act, a prototypical hero of that elevated consciousness in which:

> . . . the native hue of resolution
> Is sicklied o'er with the pale cast of
>   thought.
> (*Hamlet*, III, i, 84–85)

Different from all these, but in our time perhaps the most far-reaching effect of the hero's shadow, is the figure of the antihero. There are several species of antihero: some are repelled both by the idea of greatness and by those who exemplify it. Others are frightened by greatness; still others, bored. All these antiheroes share a conviction that heroism is not for them, but rather an ambition, a fate to be avoided.

Perhaps the best literary portrait of the antihero is Prufrock in Eliot's poem, "The Love Song of J. Alfred Prufrock." A weak, sensitive, and timid man, but conscious of heroism in human life, he occasionally contemplates doing something that might, for him, amount to an heroic act. But he constantly sinks back, with an ironic sigh, into passivity.

> No! I am not Prince Hamlet, nor was meant to be;
> Am an attendant lord, one that will do
> To swell a progress, start a scene or two . . .
> (Eliot 1940, p. 8)

Prufrock knows there is an "overwhelming question," but asks us not to ask it and instead, in his stream of consciousness, we find a portrait of the failing society which, he is convinced, has no use for serious questions. When all is said and done, he is conversing with himself, alone. His final realization is the fading of his life and his approaching death. Not daring to disturb the universe, he draws back from the seductive forces of life beckoning the hero, the same sirens who sang to Odysseus:

> I grow old, I grow old.
> I shall wear the bottoms of my trousers
>   rolled.
> Do I dare to eat a peach?
> I shall wear white flannel trousers, and walk
>   upon the beach.
> I have heard the mermaids singing, each to
>   each.
> I do not think that they will sing to me.
> (Ibid., p. 7)

The mermaids sang to Achilles and to David, to Sam Houston and Kelsey; and, terrible as their song may have been, the mermaids sang to Hitler, and to Lady Macbeth, to Stalin and to Lucrezia Borgia. With a certain self-pity and resignation, the antihero says sadly, "I do not think that they will sing to me."

The spirit of the antihero dominated students in the sixties and early seventies. Motivated by foolish and jejune conceptualizations such as Charles Reich's (1976) *Greening of America* (if Prufrock is the finest literary embodiment of the antihero, Reich is surely the finest academic embodiment), they sat like first-century Montanists on a hillside smoking pot and waiting for Consciousness III—people for whom the only law of nature was the second law of thermodynamics. They were living out the myth of the antihero. And the result could only be—can only be—the discovery that Prufrock makes: that one's time is gone, one's mortality has presented its claim. What they found was the opportunity to be preternaturally inconsequential, to achieve a precocious obscurity. Such a person lives, gropes, and dies within the shadow of the hero.

The tragedy of Prufrock and those like him is that the mermaids may in fact be singing to them, but they simply fail to hear the song. This is a tragedy for them personally; it means that they are forever prisoners of the impotence of irony. But it is an even greater tragedy for our democratic society which must have leadership in order to survive.

There is truth, of course, in what Prufrock felt, truth in the antihero. Whitehead's notion of the completely developed man—a central idea in defining the democratic hero—must include the sense of how short our lives are, how bounded—of how little we actually matter.

Our consideration of the shadow of the hero brings us to a related question, central to the concept of the democratic hero. How does an individual, aware of his finitude, his unimportance, his mortality, achieve that sense of greatness that is the motivating force of life?

Regrettably for us all, the question is more apt to be avoided than answered. The most common means of avoiding it is to abandon consciousness altogether in the mindless pursuit of pleasure. In thrall to hedonism, cut off from past and future, a disconnected present is all that remains of human life. Even when hedonism is pursued as Don Giovanni pursues it, with cosmic intensity, it betrays the final emptiness of the antihero, ending necessarily in futility. The poverty and paucity of meaning negate any notion of the heroic.

Another method of avoiding consciousness of the problem is deliberate denial of individuality. The denier feels no envy of the heroic personality; he is beyond the shadow of any individual greatness. I have in mind the "Marxist hero": he renounces all claim to, indeed all belief in, individual effort or worth; he finds his place within the historical dialectic. History for him is made not by individuals, but by dialectical forces operating through social classes. He submerges himself, not merely *accepting* his destiny as an obscure member of society, but also *seeking* this as his fulfillment. The Marxist theorist Plekhanov describes him well:

> He not only serves as an instrument of necessity and cannot help doing so, but he passionately desires this, and cannot help desiring to do so. This is an aspect of freedom. (1940, p. 17)

Orwell could not have invented a finer example of doublethink.

The Marxist playwright Bertolt Brecht reveals much more of the truth of communism than he perhaps intended when he has a disappointed follower of Galileo say: "Unhappy is the land that breeds no hero." Brecht's Galileo, who bears little if any resemblance to Galileo Galilei, replies, "No, Andreas. Unhappy is the land that needs a hero" (Brecht 1966, p. 115). Brecht's Galileo might be happy in a world in which the last brave man is dead—but only after the revolution. This will, of course, depend not on those trapped in the dialectic of history, but on those individuals who direct an elitist party structure, who tax the ordinary citizen into poverty in order to sustain armed forces that threaten the peace of the world and seek to extend the revolution of mass-man everywhere.

But for those who refuse to abandon either consciousness or individuality, who thus reject the nostrums of hedonism and Marxism, the problem of the heroic remains and must be confronted. The democratic man in his ordinariness must find that sense of greatness on which moral achievement depends. If he is not motivated by greatness in the abstract, he must be able to appropriate a model relevant to himself—a man like Jefferson, whose greatness includes a refinement and a reach which to some seems beyond that of the common man; or a man like Sam Houston, whose greatness was expressed not only in heroic appetite, ambition, and achievement, but in a magnanimity and a common touch that endeared him to Indians, Mexicans, blacks, frontiersmen, and French aristocrats.

Any number of stories might be told of Sam Houston and his effect on friends and enemies. He and other figures of Texas history and legend demonstrate that Texas has never been antihero country. The official motto of Texas is "Friendship." A more appropriate motto might be that which, from the nineteenth century well into the twentieth, was a standard text for Texas schoolchildren: *Per aspera ad astra* (through hardships to the stars). The man who said that Texas had few if any shortcomings but plenty of overdoers was not far from the mark.

The democratic hero, as these examples show, must be a multifarious man. His consciousness embraces many things; he is a man who, as Pericles said, "does many things well." He is not, and cannot be, simply a man equal to other men. American democracy is founded, as Jefferson put it, on a natural aristocracy. The democratic hero must steer a course between the worship of force and the rejection of violence. Finally, he must attempt to cope with the shadows cast by heroes present and past, and by himself.

We have come full circle here, for the democratic man in his ordinariness must discover that sense of greatness on which, as Whitehead says, moral achievement depends.

The democratic hero remains, as he must, a paradox. For all their greatness, Jefferson, Houston and the heroes of the Alamo, like all other men, were subject to the "discourtesy of death"—the ultimate democracy. The democratic hero, like all heroes however great, shares the mortality and limitation that attend all human endeavor. He lives not only in the great light of his significance—of which he may, like

Sophocles's heroes, be unconscious, though we are not—but also in the stark realization of his insignificance.

This duality is eloquent in the great chorus of Sophocles's *Antigone*, which emphasizes both the brevity of man's life and the glory of his accomplishments on earth:

> Numberless are the world's wonders, but none
> More wonderful than man; the stormgray sea
> Yields to his prows, the huge crests bear him
>   high.
> Earth, holy and inexhaustible, is graven
> With shining furrows where his plows have gone
> Year after year, the timeless labors of
>   stallions.
> Words also, and thoughts as rapid as air
> He fashions to his good use; statecraft is
>   his,
> And his the skill that deflects the arrows of
>   snow,
> The spears of winter rain; from every wind
> He has made himself secure—from all but
>   one:
> In the late wind of death he cannot stand.

It reaches us also from the Bible, from which the psalmist pronounces man's insignificance:

> As for man, his days are like grass; as a flower
>   of the field, so he flourisheth.
> For the wind passeth over it, and it is gone; and
>   the place thereof shall know it no more.
> (Psalms 103:15–16)

And from another psalmist, who invokes man's glory:

> What is man, that thou art mindful of him?
> Or the son of man, that thou visitest him?
> For thou hast made him a little lower than
>   the angels,
> And hast crowned him with glory and honor.
> Thou madest him to have dominion over the
>   works of thy hands.
> Thou hast put all things under his feet.
> (Psalms 8:4–6)

Or, once again, from Job:

> Man, that is born of woman,
> Is of few days, and full of trouble.
> He cometh forth like a flower, and is cut
>   down;
> He fleeth also as a shadow, and continueth
>   not.
> (Job 14:1–2)

It reaches us from the Gospel of St. Mark, where Jesus tells His followers that in the kingdom of heaven "many that are first shall be last and the last first." Mark also tells how:

> There came one running, and kneeled to him and
>   asked him, "Good Master, what must I do to gain
>   eternal life?"
> And Jesus said unto him, "Why callest thou me
>   good? There is none good but one, that is
>   God."
> (Mark 10:31, 10:17–28)

This humility, the humility of Jesus as true man, is counterbalanced in the Gospel of St. John where Jesus claims to be true God:

> Thomas saith unto him, "Lord, we know not whither
>   thou goest; and how can we know the way?"
> Jesus saith unto him, "I am the way, the truth,
>   and the life. No man cometh unto the Father but
>   by me."
> (John 14:5–7)

This Christian paradox offers a profound expression of the union of incompatibles. We are to be at once humbler than the lowest, but at the same time exalted by our share in the life of God. Jesus, "very God and very man," as the *Book of Common Prayer* has it, unites these opposites, reconciles human frailty and mortality to divine greatness and immortality. The least of men may be the Christian hero. There has never been a more democratic conception.

This paradox confronts not only ancient Greeks and characters from the Bible, but also twentieth-century Americans—most powerfully, I think, in the climax of Arthur Miller's *Death of a Salesman*. This play, I was told by a Yale professor, could not be a tragedy. Why? Because tragedies had to do with heroes, and Willy Loman was just an ordinary fellow who failed because he was a bad salesman. Yet for Miller the life and death of a salesman is worthy of the highest art. It is about us, and we should not be ashamed to read it and to weep honest tears of recognition.

We find ourselves voicing both sides of that climactic scene between Willy Loman and his son, Biff, where Biff, out of a life of failure, tells his father:

> Pop! I'm a dime a dozen, and so are you!

And Willy replies:

> I am not a dime a dozen! I am Willy Loman, and you are Biff Loman!

Then Biff, at the peak of his fury:

> Pop, I'm nothing! I'm nothing, Pop! Can't you understand that?

Biff collapses in tears, and Willy says:

> What're you doing? What're you doing [He turns to his wife and asks] Why is he crying? . . . Isn't that remarkable? Biff—he likes me! . . . He . . . cried to me.

Then Willy, choking with his love, cries out his promise:

> That boy—That boy is going to be magnificent! (Miller 1949, pp. 132–133)

We do not have to choose between Biff and Willy. Both are right. They are a dime a dozen, and they are magnificent. The great fact about human beings is that we are both dime a dozen and magnificent. If we believe only that we are magnificent, we become insufferably arrogant at best; at worst, Tamburlaines. On the other hand if we believe that we are merely dime a dozen, we lose our reason for being, the motivation for excellence and the ability to sustain the disappointments and losses that go with even the happiest and most fortunate of lives. Heroism is not only essential to democracy, it is essential to the life of every human being. The genius of democracy is found in this paradox: that we are all a dime a dozen and that we are all magnificent. The democratic hero is not an ideal beyond our grasp; it is relevant and compelling to each of us.

We know from looking about us that wisdom is within the reach of anyone, for some of the simplest human beings are wise. Virtue is within the reach of anyone, for some of the least educated are good. Happiness is within the reach of anyone, for some of the poorest are happy. There is neither a positive nor a negative correlation between intelligence, learning, and wealth on the one hand and wisdom, virtue, and happiness on the other.

The mermaids sing each to each, and they sing to each of us. But not all of us hear their song.

Why should we resign ourselves to insignificance and forfeit our promise of greatness? Unless, in the words of Augie March, "you want to say that we're at the dwarf end of all times, and mere children whose only share in grandeur is like a boy's share in fairy-tale kings, beings of a different kind from times better and stronger than ours" (Bellow 1953, p. 60).

In Texas, as contrasted with other parts of the United States, it is unlikely that men and women shall fail because they are overcome by a sense of modesty or ordinariness. Texans are not merely dime a dozen. They are not Prufrocks to whom the mermaids will never sing. Texans err on the side of ambition. If the mermaids will sing to anyone, they will sing to them. Their motivation for greatness has not been eclipsed by mortal thoughts. In Texas, the myth of the hero has abiding appeal.

References

Bellow, Saul. 1970. *Mr. Sammler's Planet*. New York: Viking Press.

———. 1953. *The Adventures of Augie March*. New York: Viking Press.

Brecht, Bertolt. 1966. *Galileo*. Translated by Charles Laughton. New York: Grove Press.

Eliot, T. S. 1940. *The Waste Land and Other Poems*. London: Faber and Faber.

Herford, C. H. and Percy Simpson, eds. 1932. *Ben Jonson: Works*, vol. 5. London: Oxford University Press.

Hill, J. W. 1888. *Amateur Etchings of Texas Character and Else*. Greenville, Texas. Reprinted in Mody C. Boatright, *Folk Laughter on the American Frontier* (New York: Collier Books, 1961).

Keynes, W., ed. 1966. *Blake: Complete Writings*. London: Oxford University Press.

Lewis, A. H. 1902. *Wolfville Days*. New York: Stokes.

Luke, D., ed. 1964. *Goethe: Selected Verse*. New York: Penguin Books.

Miller, Arthur. 1949. *The Death of a Salesman*. New York: Viking Press.

Pierson, G. W. 1938. *Tocqueville and Beaumont in America*. New York: Oxford University Press.

Plekhanov, G. 1940. *The Role of the Individual in History*. New York: International Publishers.

Reich, Charles. 1976. *The Greening of America: How the Youth Revolution Is Trying to Make America Livable.* New York: Random House.

School Document No. 6–1884: Report of the Committee on Textbooks; School Document No. 15–1884: Report of the Committee on Textbooks on Supplementary Reading, October 1884; School Document No. 11–1884: List of Authorized Text and Reference Books for School Year 1884–85. Boston: Rockwell and Churchill, City Printers, 1884.

Smith, C. B. 1928. Diplomatic Relations Between the United States and Mexico over Border Disturbances During the Diaz Regime—1876–1910. Masters dissertation. Austin: University of Texas.

Sophocles. 1958. *The Oedipus Cycle: An English Version by Dudley Fitts and Robert Fitzgerald.* New York: Harcourt Brace.

Webb, W. P. 1935. *The Texas Rangers: A Century of Frontier Defense.* Boston: Houghton Mifflin Co.

Whitehead, A. N. 1949. *Aims of Education.* New York: New American Library.

CHAPTER
NINE

Jung: Father and Son—One View

Murray Stein

A paper entitled "The Significance of Jung's Father in His Destiny as a Therapist of Christianity," presented at the National Conference of Jungian Analysts, New York, May 3–6, 1984. Reprinted with permission of the C. G. Jung Foundation for Analytical Psychology as published in "Quadrant," vol. 18, no. 1 (Spring 1985), pp. 23–33.

About Murray Stein

Murray Stein first came upon C. G. Jung's thought by accident when, at the age of 16 and a high school student in Detroit, Michigan, he happened to find a volume entitled *Psychology and Religion* in a local library. Without understanding much of its content, he nevertheless felt strongly drawn to the subject and hoped to be able to pursue it one day. The chapter included in this book is an adaptation of a chapter from his book *Jung's Treatment of Christianity*, which represents the fulfilment of this dream of adolescence. The work is the fruit of a union between two disciplines, psychology and religious studies, both of which have been central to Stein's interests since childhood.

Like Jung, Stein is the son of a Protestant pastor. Upon graduating from Yale College with a B.A. in English, he walked for a time in his father's footsteps, attending Yale Divinity School and considering the ministry as a vocation. While there he rediscovered the work of C. G. Jung and chose to become a Jungian analyst, enrolling at the C. G. Jung Institute of Zürich. His mentor at the time, Russell Becker, professor of practical theology at Yale, served as a model for combining the interests in pastoral care and psychotherapy with a depth psychological orientation. After graduating from the Jung Institute in 1973, Murray was ordained a Presbyterian minister in Houston, Texas, where he taught and practiced Jungian analysis until moving to Chicago in 1976 and enrolling in the doctoral program at the University of Chicago in religion and psychological studies. *Jung's Treatment* is the product of those years of study and reflection.

In addition to the work already cited, Murray has written *In Midlife*, a book about the midlife transition, and has edited many volumes, including *Jungian Analysis* and *Jung's Challenge to Contemporary Religion* (with Robert Moore).

Jung's was a childhood spent in large and poorly furnished manses, without the company of siblings or playmates. His mother seemed to have two different personalities, a conventional "day-personality" and an uncanny "night-personality" (Jung 1961, pp. 48–49). His father, while reliable, was a powerless man and was unable to help him overcome his childhood fears and somatic symptoms (ibid., p. 8).

His early preoccupation with religion and religious questions, as attested in his memoirs, seems extremely precocious, but this took place in the context of family life in the *Pharrhaus,* which Brome refers to as "one of the germinal cells of German culture" (Brome 1978, p. 28). In Jung's case, it was more than usually occupied by the influence and presence of the Protestant church. On his mother's side, there were six uncles who were parsons and a famous parson grandfather, Samuel Preiswerk (1799–1871), who had been *Antistes* of Basel, a position roughly equivalent to that of an English bishop (Hannah 1976, p. 21). (This gentleman, whom Jung never knew but who was the subject of many stories in the family and beyond, was said to have engaged in the extraordinary practice of consulting weekly with the spirit of his deceased first wife, in the presence of his understandably jealous and resentful second wife, Jung's grandmother (Brome 1978, p. 24). On his father's side, there were two more parson uncles. As far as the child's eye could see, there were staunch representatives of the Swiss Protestant church.

Thus, the intensity and extent of Jung's early preoccupation with religious figures and thoughts are striking, but understandable, under these circumstances. In the earliest years, moreover, before he had reached the age of five, a series of images and experiences came together that set the stage for his profound and lifelong ambivalence toward many basic elements of Christianity. This nexus of emotionally charged material—the breeding ground for what I call Jung's Christianity complex—was made of memory images of pious men in black coats burying corpses of children, of threatening Jesuits in black dress, and of references to a Lord Jesus who, the child discovered, was wont to steal children like himself from their homes while they slept.

At the center of his Christianity complex, beside his early suspicion of Lord Jesus and his sense of God's dark side, stood Jung's own father. Johann Paul Achilles Jung (1842–1896) was a pastor in the Swiss Reformed Church. The youngest son of a famous and very impressive Basel professor of medicine, Carl Gustav Jung (1794–1864), Paul Jung studied theology and took a doctorate in Oriental languages at Gottingen University. Thereafter he served pastorates in Kesswil on Lake Constance, where Carl was born in 1875; in Laufen, a village on the

Rheinfall near Schaffhausen some fifty miles north of Zürich on the Swiss-German border; and after 1879, until his death, in Klein-Hüningen, near Basel, where he also served as chaplain to the Freidmatt Mental Hospital. As Jung saw him from a later vantage point, he was a weak man. After glorious days as a student in a renowned Germany university, he "lapsed into a sort of sentimental idealism and into reminiscences of his golden student days" (Jung 1961, p. 91). Sadly, as his son saw it, his life had "come to a standstill at his graduation" (ibid., p. 95). After that, scholarship and professional ambition had apparently left him, and while he performed the conventional role of pastor, doing "a great deal of good—far too much," his emotional and spiritual life had gone dead (ibid., p. 215).

For Jung, issues that began with a weak father image expanded into far broader territory. In the son's mind, the father's weakness and suffering could not be cleanly separated from his identity as a pastor and from his commitment to living spiritually within the Christian tradition. Jung later held Christianity partly accountable for his father's plight, but held his father accountable as well. The father had shirked the task of struggling with the great spiritual issues of the age, issues that his son would have to take up: the conflicts between tradition and modernity and between science and religion. While Paul Jung suffered the spiritual plight of modern man dumbly and blindly, his son Carl Gustav would take it on as a conscious problem in desperate need of resolution. Healing the spiritual sources of his father's suffering became in many ways Jung's vocation.

In old age Jung recounted the kernel of his memory of a father who had died some sixty years earlier, yet who lived vividly in his son's psyche: "My memory of my father is of a sufferer stricken with an Amfortas wound, a 'fisher king' whose wound would not heal—that Christian suffering for which the alchemists sought the panacea. I as a 'dumb' Parsifal was witness of this sickness during the years of my boyhood, and, like Parsifal, speech failed me. I had only inklings" (ibid.). What this "Amfortas wound" was, and what this "Christian suffering," will be discussed later; what is essential to recognize here is the lifelong impact this sense of his father's woundedness made on Jung. His conviction, at which he arrived around age seventeen, was that his father's relationship to Christianity was at the center of his suffering; his father was both representative and victim of an ailing religious tradition.

The sense of his father's weakness reached a climax during Jung's early adolescence, when the lad's struggles with Christian theology and doctrine had reached a high level of intensity; this was around the time of his confirmation. Later Jung wrote that he realized even then that "the church is a place I should not go to. It is not life which is there, but death. . . . All at once I understood the tragedy of his [i.e., father's] profession and his life. He was struggling with a death whose existence he could not admit" (ibid., p. 55).

What Jung found so utterly lacking in his father was the sense of God's immediate presence and reality. There was no sense of God's grace. His father, as Jung saw it, "had taken the Bible's commandments as his guide; he believed in God as the Bible prescribed and as his forefathers had taught him. But he did not know the immediate living God who stands, omnipotent and free, above His Bible and His Church . . ." (ibid., p. 40). Jung's father was intellectually and emotionally committed to traditional Swiss Protestant forms of belief and practice; he refused either to question this position in the light of modern thought or to step outside of it to gain a firsthand experience of the source of spiritual life. "Faith" was an act of willful belief in traditional teachings. In the end, Jung felt that "faith broke faith with him" and left him stranded on the shores of a spiritual wasteland, without any resources for renewal.

Jung's scandalous fantasy of the Basel cathedral destroyed by God (ibid., p. 36ff), and his interpretation that God made him create the fantasy, produced a sense of grace, but it also reinforced his early childhood sense of God's dark side. This topic was not much contemplated in his home or in the homes of his ministerial relatives. The boy felt he could not share his religious questions with his father, because his father "would be obliged to reply out of respect for his office" (ibid., p. 52), and therefore would be of no help. Church became "a place of torment," so keen was Jung's conviction that he had seen God, and a deeply hidden, unacknowledged side of Him at that.

When the time came for Jung to take his first communion, the banality of the church was what struck him most forcefully. His verdict was that the communion "did not compare at all with secular festivals" (ibid., p. 54). Mostly, old men were present, "stiff, solemn, and, it seemed to me, uninterested" (ibid.). The ceremony was traditional and correct, the bread poor in quality, the wine thin and sour. In the days following this event, it gradually dawned on the boy that "nothing at all had happened" (ibid.). What had been confirmed was the boy's feeling that the church was a place of death. And, with that conviction now in place, he wrote, "I was seized with the most vehement pity for my father" (ibid., p. 55). This was Jung's first deep glimpse into what he would later call his father's "Amfortas wound."

While this experience convinced Jung that he was outside the boundaries of Christian religion (ibid., p. 56), he nonetheless felt empathy for those who, like his father, could not afford to face their inner truths and be plunged "into that despair and sacrilege which were necessary for an experience of divine grace" (ibid., p. 55). Later, as he came to understand his early life experiences, Jung realized that the Cathedral fantasy had taught him that even as faith had broken faith with his father, so "God Himself had disavowed theology and the Church founded upon it" (ibid., p. 93). Thus, his father's desperate situation also reflected the whole Christian Church's situation: both were abandoned by God and left stranded on dry shores without spiritual resource.

Jung also analyzed his father's predicament from another, related viewpoint that was more cognitive. The central issue was Paul Jung's refusal to engage in the contemporary conflict created by the emotional and intellectual claims of tradition versus those of modernity. He committed a *sacrificium intellectus*, and this, combined with his lack of primary religious experience, had produced his sadly crippled emotional and intellectual existence. The adult Jung saw the tragedy of a man clinging stubbornly to the sinking vessel of traditional Christian forms in the swift currents of modernity.

After his fifteenth or sixteenth year Jung's interests gradually shifted away from religion and theology to other areas, and by his nineteenth year he was giving priority to the natural sciences and to certain pagan philosophers such as Pythagoras, Heraclitus, and Plato rather than Christian theologians and philosophers. His depressions waned, and he looked forward to pursuing these new interests at the University of Basel.

When the time came for Jung to choose a course of study, his father had "serious talks" with him. "Be anything you like except a theologian" (ibid., p. 75), was the message. In addition to warning his son about his own professional pitfall, Jung's father also indicated his ambivalence by allowing the son to lapse from church attendance. Young Carl was delighted and missed nothing but the music. As for church-goers, he disliked them especially, an attitude not uncommon among "preacher's kids" everywhere, in every time.

At the time of Jung's entry into the University of Basel, then, one would have expected this youth to be more or less completely alienated from Christianity and from the church of his Swiss-Protestant father, family, and forebears. And yet he carried into university life, perhaps under a seemingly indifferent appearance, the spiritual problems that his father and his father's religion had raised so acutely in his earlier years. Looking back later on his first twenty-one years of life from the vantage point of old age, Jung perceived a direct relationship between his own youthful religious experiences and struggles and the difficulties his father was having at the same time with Christian faith. He wrote:

> Children react much less to what grown-ups say than to the imponderables in the surrounding atmosphere. The peculiar "religious" ideas that came to me even in earliest childhood were spontaneous products which can be understood only as reactions to my parental environment and to the spirit of the age. The religious doubts to which my father was later to succumb naturally had to pass through a long period of incubation. Such a revolution of one's world, and of the world in general, threw its shadows ahead, and the shadows were all the longer, the more desperately my father's conscious mind resisted their power. (Ibid., p. 90)

Jung's religious experiences represented a compensatory reaction from the unconscious: the youth was carrying the burden of an answer from the unconscious to the spiritual dilemmas faced both by his father and by others who, like his father, were falling victim to the cultural crisis.

Paul Jung died in 1896, when Carl was twenty-one and still a student at the University. In Jung's later view, it was a tragic death, directly attributable to his father's conflicts. But only after looking back over some sixty years did Jung come to this final understanding of his father's suffering and its meaning. At the time of the event, he had little of this awareness and knew only that there was a cleavage between himself and his father. He had continued raising troublesome questions about Christian belief, and his father was unable to provide answers that were adequate for himself or his son. Carl Jung began to sense something deeply amiss in his father, and eventually he surmised that his father was suffering from "religious doubts." Observing this suffering, a Parsifal to an Amfortas, he stood helplessly by and watched the agony unfold. He could not speak the healing words, since his own experience of God's grace was taboo:

> This was a great secret which I dared not and could not reveal to my father. I might have been able to reveal it had he been capable of understanding the direct experience of God. But in my talks with him I never got that far, never even came within sight of the problem, because I always set about it in a very unpsychological and intellectual way, and did everything to avoid the emotional aspects. (Ibid., p. 93)

Finally, the discussions broke down altogether and Jung concluded that "Theology had alienated my father and me from one another" (ibid.). His father was entrapped in the Church's thinking about God (its "theology") and consequently could not allow himself to experience God directly. "Now I understood the deepest meaning of my earlier experience," Jung wrote, referring to the cathedral-breaking fantasy:

"God Himself had disavowed theology and the Church founded upon it" (ibid.). "Theological religion," as Jung called it, was hollow, a dead letter and largely responsible for his father's pitiful condition and early demise.

What perhaps horrified Jung even more, however, was the direction his father took to seek aid. Instead of looking to religion—the real source of his anguish—for answers to his doubts, he turned to "the ridiculous materialism of the psychiatrists!" While chaplain at the Friedmatt Mental Hospital, Paul Jung began reading Sigmund Freud's translation of Bernheim's work *Die Suggestion und Ihre Heilwirkung*. But in looking to psychiatry for answers to religious questions, the father was, in the opinion of his son, leaping from the frying pan into the fire. Psychiatry was one of the ultimate statements of the antireligious, materialistic attitude of modernity. At most, it could soothe the surface of consciousness, but fundamentally its answers to religious questions would be anathema to the religious spirit. In despair over faith, Paul Jung ironically was seeking help from the very forces that had participated in creating his crisis of faith.

Jung observed that his father's "psychiatric reading made him no happier. His depressive moods increased in frequency and intensity, and so did his hypochondria" (ibid., p. 94). The solution to a spiritual problem must derive from the spiritual realm, Jung felt, not from the rationalistic notions hatched in the medium of modern materialism. But Paul Jung's "faith" made a spiritual approach to his crisis impossible, for this would have required that he relinquish his traditional beliefs about God and enter the terrifying realm of firsthand religious experience.

Pastor Jung began to complain that he had "stones in the abdomen," and within months he was a complete invalid. It was a great wound to his self-esteem that now "Carl had to carry him round like a heap of bones for an anatomy class" (Oeri 1970, pp. 182–189). While the medical diagnosis remained uncertain, it quickly became clear that Paul Jung was fading rapidly from life.

Jung was at his father's bedside when he died. His detached clinical observation of the scene bespeaks his ambivalence toward the dying pastor, and it seems an obvious defense against the awareness of what was certainly a chilling denouement to his father's ill-fated existence: "There was a rattling in his throat, and I could see that he was in the death agony. I stood by his bed, fascinated. I had never seen anyone die before. Suddenly he stopped breathing. I waited and waited for the next breath. It did not come" (Jung 1961, p. 96). From then on, Jung would contend with his father, and with the source of his father's illness, only in his own spirit and in his dreams.

In *Memories, Dreams, Reflections,* Jung recorded three dreams about his father in detail and summarized several others. Elsewhere, some further details about these have come to light and still other dreams about his father are mentioned (see Bennet 1982). The first of the father dreams recorded in *Memories* occurred early and is related to Jung's description of his father's death. Carl, twenty-one at the time, had moved into his father's vacant bedroom, and there he had a recurring anxiety dream: His father was coming home and would find him occupying his room. In these dreams, the victorious Oedipal son (his mother had said to Jung shortly after her husband's death, "He died in time for you"!) (Jung 1961, p. 96) was frightened and ashamed. His father was not angry at him, however; he had recovered from his illness and was simply coming home again. Later Jung interpreted these dreams as indications of what was transpiring with his father in the afterlife (ibid.).

The next dream, recorded in more detail, was fixed to a precise date in Jung's memory. It occurred in 1922, just a few weeks prior to his mother's death. Jung had not dreamed of his father since 1896, he noted in *Memories.* In this dream, Paul Jung appeared as having just returned from a long journey, rejuvenated and without the aura of paternal authority. Carl was thrilled to see his father again and eager to relate to him everything he had accomplished in his absence; particularly, he wanted to tell him about his recently published book, *Psychological Types.* But it turned out that his father had come for a professional consultation: he wanted some information and advice about marriage! After his mother's death a few weeks later, Jung took this dream as premonitory. His father had been preparing himself to resume a relationship with his wife "on the other side" and wanted some advice about how to improve what had formerly been a difficult marriage.

This dream picture of Paul Jung coming to his son for assistance, and in effect asking for therapy, is of a piece with the picture of the son carrying his broken father in strong arms during the last months of his life. Both scenes indicate the achievement of a countertransference position in Jung's attitude toward the paternal. The son is doctor to his father's patienthood; the father is patient to his son's doctoring.

The other two major father dreams recorded in *Memories* were placed some two to three decades later. One took place in the early 1940s, the other around 1950. These two dreams are much more symbolic than the earlier ones; they also give somewhat more indication of the substantive issues about the Christian care of souls and Christian theology.

The first of these should be placed in the context of Jung's life in the early 1940s. Despite the terrifying reality of war in Europe and the constant threat of invasion to Switzerland, Jung undertook lecturing and writing with added intensity during this period (Hannah 1976). There was additional free time in his practice and he felt burdened with much still to say and write. The central themes in his lecturing and writing were explicitly associated with the Christian tradition. The two major works of these early war years are evidence of this new focus: "A Psychological Approach to the Dogma of the Trinity" (begun as a spontaneous lecture at the Eranos Conference in 1940, then revised and published in 1942) and "Transformation Symbolism in the Mass" (given as an Eranos lecture in 1941 and published in 1942). Jung had never before written an essay focused exclusively on Christian doctrine or rite, and these two papers would be the forerunners of much similar material to come. Jung identified the first of his two late father dreams as a "herald" of what was to come.

The dream ran as follows: Jung discovers a large wing of his house never visited before, which contains a zoological laboratory. This belongs to his father, it turns out, and is his workroom. His father is an ichthyologist, and the workroom contains every kind of fish imaginable. Then Hans, a country boy, shows Jung still another room. This one belongs to his mother. Two rows of chests hang from the ceiling; each chest contains two beds for visiting spirits ("ghostly married couples") to sleep in. Another door is opened, and Jung finds a brass band loudly playing dance tunes and marches in a large hall. He is struck, in the dream itself, by the strong contrast between the different spiritual mysteries in the silent inner chambers (Jung 1961, p. 213–214).

Possibly more important than this dream itself, which shows up so well the split in Jung's personality between his jovial, extraverted Personality Number One and his mystical, introverted Personality Number Two, is the interpretation he gave it. He found that it confirmed his vocation as a healer of Christian souls and a therapist to the Christian tradition.

Jung took the idea that his father was an ichthyologist as a reflection of his father's actual identity as a Christian pastor, a "caretaker of Christian souls" who had been caught in "Peter's net." The fish represented the souls in a pastor's keeping. His mother, too, was evidently "burdened with the problem of the 'cure of souls' " in the dream (ibid., p. 214). This dream, Jung felt, put the burden of the care and cure of Christian souls squarely on his own shoulders. The presence of the parent imagos symbolized his own unconsciousness and the parents' tasks represented the work he still had to do. The tasks were still latent in his unconscious and were now beginning to reveal themselves. This was the meaning of the "discovery motif" in the dream.

Jung's further associations to "fish" led him to reflect on the Grail legend and the "fisher king," which in turn aroused the thought of his father as "a sufferer stricken with an Amfortas wound." The type of suffering that Jung saw in his father's life exemplified "that Christian suffering for which the alchemists sought the panacea" (ibid., p. 215): this was the suffering of wounded souls whose access to "nature" and to its healing properties had been cut off.

Jung himself was deeply immersed in the study of alchemy at this time. For him, alchemy came to represent the equivalent in Western European tradition of his own analytical psychology in modernity (ibid., p. 212). Both worked outside the collective mainstream, and each was searching for the *lumen naturae*, the hidden sparks of consciousness ("light") within the depths of the unconscious ("nature"). The conviction took hold in Jung that his own work, a psychology of the unconscious, was an effort akin to the alchemists' search for a panacea, a quest to find a therapeutic release for the suffering of souls caught in the net of a one-sided, strangulating Christian tradition. This was the same net that had ensnared and eventually strangled his own father's spirit.

Around 1950, Jung noted in his memoirs (ibid., p. 217ff), he had another major dream in which his father again played a key role. If the earlier dream of his parents' "soul-curing rooms" presaged his work on the Christian tradition in *Aion* (1951) and in his *magnum opus, Mysterium Coniunctionis* (1955), this latter dream prefigured the central theme of *Answer to Job* (1952), the work that of all Jung's writings most clearly expressed his intensely emotional relationship to Christianity and its central symbol, the Godhead. Again, as this dream and Jung's interpretation of it clearly demonstrate, his relationship to his father and his relationship to Christianity and its theology were deeply intertwined, even at the advanced age of seventy-five.

In this dream, Jung is paying a visit to his long-deceased father. Again his father is a curator, not of fish this time but of an eighteenth-century mansion that contains the sarcophagi of famous personages. He is also a distinguished scholar. Two other psychiatrists are present as well. His father takes a heavy old Bible bound in shiny fish skin from a shelf and begins interpreting a passage from the Pentateuch, but so swift and learned is his exposition that Jung and the other two psychiatrists cannot follow it. In fact, the intensity and excitement of the flood of ideas pouring into his mind leads the other two psychiatrists to suspect a pathological condition. (These figures, Jung commented, represent the limited medical viewpoint, which was an aspect of his own "shadow," a twentieth-century bourgeois rationalist!)

Then the scene changes. Father and son are outside, in front of the house, and they hear noises in a nearby shed. Jung's father says the shed is haunted by poltergeists. Entering the house again, they come into a large second-story hall, "the exact replica of the *divan-i-kass* (council hall) of Sultan Akbar of Fatehpur Sikri." The room is circular, in the shape of a mandala. At the center, on an elevated base, is the seat of the sultan; around the rim are seats for his counselors and for the court philosophers. From the raised center there is a steep stairway that leads to a small door high up on the wall. His father points to it and says, "Now I will lead you into the highest presence," then he kneels and touches his head to the floor Moslem style. Jung follows suit, but his head does not go all the way to the floor; there remains "perhaps a millimeter to spare." It suddenly dawns on Jung that this door leads to the chamber of Uriah, King David's betrayed general (ibid.).

Again, it is as much Jung's interpretation of this dream as the dream itself that is important. His father, who had been trained as a scholar of near-Eastern languages but had not used his education productively in his pastoral career, is associated in the dream with the biblical tradition. In fact, in this dream he is seen as the scholar he never became in life. Upon reflection, Jung interpreted this image of his father, who is so intensely engrossed in interpreting and understanding the Bible, as a signal that his own unconscious was engaged in this task. Here lay his own unfinished business: interpreting the Christian God-image in the light of its Semitic, Old Testament background.

By the time this dream occurred, Jung had already been engaged in interpreting Christianity for some ten years, but he had not paid particular attention to the Old Testament background. This dream anticipated *Answer to Job*, which was to be a passionate interpretation (*à la* dream-father!) of the God-image in Judaism (Yahweh), its transformation in Christianity, its evolution in the two Christian millennia following, and its future.

This dream's second major point of significance for Jung lay in the contrast drawn between the attitudes of father and son toward the "holy." In bowing to the "highest presence," his father's head touches the floor, indicating complete submission and trust; Carl's head, however, does not quite touch. Jung pointed out that this indicated a fundamental, lifelong attitude: his determination "not to be a dumb fish." Even in the presence of the sacred, he would retain a mental reservation. This, he expounded, was also precisely the stance of Job, who refused to accept his companions' conventional doctrine on sin and punishment but rather reserved judgment for himself. He even went so far as to make God answer for *His* deeds. *God* can be at fault, too, and in need of greater consciousness and further development. This commitment to the freedom and integrity of human judgment (Jung's strongest affirmation of an "ego psychology") barely disguised "the idea of the creature that surpasses its creator by a small but decisive factor." Uriah, the innocent victim and a prefiguraion of Christ, was a symbol of the same value that Job represented. And clearly, Jung himself identified with this lineage of defiant innocents, whereas his father represented the more docile (and traditional) attitude toward authority and the conventional image of God. This dream exemplified, then, Jung's attitude toward the religious tradition represented by his father: The God who is the symbolic center of this tradition's life and faith is as much in need of transformation as man. And if this tradition is to remain a vital one, its God-image must go through a transformation.

As had been the case with the other two dreams of this late period—the Holy Grail dream and the "cure of souls" dream—this dream of his father as Biblical interpreter both reflected Jung's already deep involvement with Christianity and, at the same time, strengthened his commitment to continue working at the therapy of Christianity. By now he was doing what his father had left undone: *he* was addressing himself to the cure of Christian souls and to the task of finding the panacea for Christian suffering. Also, he was interpreting the biblical tradition in the light of psychological understanding. Most of all, he was preparing to face up to the task his father had fearfully evaded—confronting the Christian tradition and its symbolic center, the Godhead, with the full force of his own personality. This he would do in *Answer to Job*.

References

Bennet, E. A. 1982. *Meetings with Jung*. London: Anchor Press.
Brome, V. 1978. *Jung: Man and Myth*. New York: Atheneum.
Hannah, B. 1976. *Jung: His Life and Work*. New York: G. P. Putnam's Sons.
Jung, C. G. 1961. *Memories, Dreams, Reflections*. New York: Random House.
Oeri, A. 1970. Some youthful memories of C. G. Jung. In *Spring* (1970): 182–189.

CHAPTER TEN

Jung: Father and Son—Another View

Harry A. Wilmer

*A paper entitled, "Jung: Father and Son,"
presented at the National Conference of
Jungian Analysts, New York, May 3–6,
1984. Reprinted with permission of the
C. G. Jung Foundation for Analytical Psychology as published in "Quadrant," vol.
18, no. 1 (Spring 1985), pp. 35–40.*

About Harry A. Wilmer

Harry Wilmer presented the following essay at the National Meeting of Jungian analysts in New York responding to Murray Stein's lecture which preceded it as it does in this book. Wilmer was asked to present his ideas on short notice because of illness of the scheduled analyst. Dr. Wilmer reacts to Jung and his father, not having known C. G. Jung himself, but having known his son Franz, and out of feelings, intuitions, and readings as well as being acquainted with many people who knew Jung or were analyzed by him. Wilmer takes a nontraditional view of the relationship, seeing the strength and love as more significant than the weaknesses and failures. And in the essay, he notes the influence of his own relationship with his father.

Harry Wilmer graduated from the University of Minnesota Medical School in 1940 and interned at the Gorgas Hospital in the Panama Canal Zone. There he contracted tuberculosis and returned to the United States where he followed a strict bed-rest cure for 11 months (there were no antibiotic drugs in 1941). He held a commission in the United States Navy and did not serve until the Korean War. He returned as a captain. While in the Sanatorium at Hopkins, Minnesota, and later at Trudeau Sanatorium, Saranac Lake, New York, he wrote and illustrated his first book, *Huber the Tuber, The Lives and Loves of a Tubercle Bacillus* which surprisingly sold almost 90,000 hardback copies. His other books followed his total recovery: *Corky the Killer; This Is Your World; Social Psychiatry in Action; The Mind—First Steps; Practical Jung; Vietnam in Remission* (co-editor); and *Facing Evil* (co-editor). He has completed a new book on Jungian psychology entitled *Understandable Jung* and has other books in progress.

Author of over 200 scientific publications, Dr. Wilmer retired from his professorship in psychiatry at the University of Texas Health Science Center at San Antonio in 1987. He previously taught at Stanford, the University of California at San Francisco, and was a consultant on the staff of the Mayo Clinic, Rochester, Minnesota. He has been awarded a Guggenheim Fellowship and a National Research Council Fellowship in the Medical Sciences at Johns Hopkins University. He holds a master's degree in anatomy and the history of medicine and also a Ph.D. in pathology. His work has focused on Jungian analysis, AIDS, Vietnam veterans with combat nightmares, therapeutic communities, television, and film. Wilmer was founder and director of the International Film Festival on Psychiatry and the Humanities at the University of Texas from 1972–1979. In 1980 he founded the Institute for the Humanities at Salado, Texas, of which he is director and president. He is a senior analyst in the Interregional Society of Jungian Analysts.

We are always disappointed by our fathers.[1] If we don't learn that lesson we never grow up—we never mature or become our "own persons."

The amount of factual information on the relationship between Carl Gustav Jung and his father is meager, and commentaries on it are surprisingly repetitious, relying on metaphors and phrases of recollections Dr. Jung made in his eighties. I do not doubt the truth of this material, but propose that there are alternative hypotheses and perspectives that bring the story into an appropriate balance. "Any view of reality, when taken to be true becomes imposing," says Santayana, and

---

[1] Fathers have disappointed their sons from time immemorial, not only in obvious matters, but sometimes subtly—for instance, by failing to bring expected messages. A number of years ago I came across a third century papyrus in the British Museum [A. P. Papyrus verso 1575 British Museum] of the following letter from Thonis to his father. Ariõ:

This is the fifth time I have written to you, and you have only written to me once, and even then you didn't say a word about yourself nor have you ever come to see me. You promised me 'I will come' but you never come to see if my teacher is looking after me properly or not. He asks himself about you almost every day: "Isn't he coming yet?' and I just say 'Yes.' So do please come as soon as possible so that he can start teaching me, which he is eager to do. If you had travelled up river with me I should have been taught long ago, and when you do come, remember all the things I have written you so often. Come quickly to us before he leaves for upper Egypt.

P.S. Remember our pigeons.

he adds, "The art of fiction may tell us truth about the fiction natural to the mind" (Santayana 1930, p. 433, 460).

The traditional story focuses on the father's shortcomings, a phenomenon that every son discovers about his father sooner or later. Murray Stein reminds us of Johann Paul Achilles as a "weak man," "shirking his task" of spiritual struggle; "refus[ing] to step outside" his "willful belief"; "stranded in a wasteland"; living a "sadly crippled" emotional and intellectual existence; "clinging stubbornly"; having an "ill-fated life"; and being "helpless and powerless." His son held "theological religion" responsible for his "pitiful condition and early demise." These are dramatic characterizations—pejorative, but perhaps just one side of the equation.

We are reminded that during his father's terminal illness Carl carried his "broken" father like "a heap of bones for an anatomy class"—not Professor Jung's metaphor, but the words of his student friend, Albert Oeri (Oeri 1970). Although Carl used the words "predictability and powerlessness" to describe his father, he was looking back more than seventy years. It must have seemed different to him as a small boy when Paul "gathered him up, struggling and kicking, to be carried forcibly to his bedroom" (Brome 1978, p. 33).

We know none of the facts and have no diagnosis of his father's fatal illness. We know only the brutal experience of his death and the inevitable ambivalence of the son and the father. For on the positive side there was a strong, caring father as well as a tender relationship. Carl wrote of "my dear and generous father, who in so many matters left me to myself, and who never tyrannized over me" (Jung 1969, p. 73).

There was also a gentle *carrying* of son and of father: Paul and Carl; Carl and Paul; and later Carl and Sigmund. One of the images that kept returning to Carl Gustav in later life was that of being carried by his father when he was very small and ill, his father singing old student songs: "One which I was especially fond of and which always soothed me, *'Alles schweige, jeder neige'* .... To this day I can remember my father's voice singing over me in the stillness of the night" (ibid., p. 22).

In 1909, when Carl Jung insisted on discussing the peat bog corpses in Bremen with Freud on their way to the United States, Freud, believing that this was a manifestation of Jung's death wish for him, the father, fainted. Jung picked up Freud and carried him in his arms. Again, in Munich in 1912, after Jung explained his idea that the Egyptian Pharaoh Akhnaton's creation of a monotheistic religion could not be accepted as a personal resistance to the father, Sigmund Freud fainted. Jung wrote, "I picked him up, carried him into the next room and laid him on a sofa. As I was carrying him, he half came to, and I shall never forget the look he cast at me. In his weakness he looked at me as if I were his father" (ibid., p. 180).

"Naturally [Freud] assumed that my more positive ideas about religion and its importance for our psychological life were nothing but an outcrop of my unrealized resistances against my clergyman father, whereas in reality my problem and my personal prejudice were never centered in my father, but most emphatically in my mother" (Jung 1975, p. 296).

The personal memory of the father is supplemented by the historical, mythological, and religious collective images in his son's psyche. Johann Paul Achilles Jung was a man of his times, and Carl Gustav Jung was a part of the *Zeitgeist* that characterized the intellectual renaissance of Basal at the end of the nineteenth century. Carl, stimulated by his father's unfulfilled, unsatisfying life, devoted his own life task, in a metaphorical sense, to the completion of his father's work. It is almost as if he had a calling to finish this mysterious labor. As Ellenberger says:

> . . . Jung emphasized not so much the son's hostility toward the father but the unconscious identification with him and the ancestors on the father's side . . . In Jung's case it seems that his religious and philosophical interests were awakened, but because he could not receive an answer that would satisfy him from his father, he turned his inquiry to other problems beyond the scope of traditional religion (Ellenberger 1970, p. 662).

It is perhaps not altogether a coincidence that Carl, reflecting on his own shadow, was to say, "My solace was always Paul, who did not deem it beneath his dignity to admit a thorn in the flesh" (Jung 1975, p. 277). In 1909 Jung wrote "The Significance of the Father in the Destiny of the Individual." He postulated that the roots of fate go deeper than the family romance, embracing the whole of humanity, and that the father imago is charged with a dynamism we cannot attribute to the individual father. The double aspects of the father imago are characteristic of the archetype in general. "Every normal human situation is provided for, and, as it were, imprinted on this inherited structure, since it has happened innumerable times before in our long ancestry. At the same time the structure brings with it an inborn tendency to seek out, or to produce, such situations instinctively" (Jung 1949, p. 302).

In the end, Carl reflected that his father "had literally lived right up to his death the suffering prefigured and promised by Christ, without ever becoming aware that his was a consequence of the *imitatio Christi*" (Jung 1969, p. 241). It was Carl who would become aware, conscious of this in his own and his father's life. Perhaps Johann Paul Achilles Jung did not so much lead a weak, pitiful, shirking, powerless life as an unexamined life—with the agony of being aware that he was not finding his way.

We can remind ourselves that his father taught Latin to Carl from the age of six, and that it was in his father's library that Jung began his scholarly education and to which he retreated when beset by doubts. He said his father was very liberal, most tolerant, and understanding.

Was Carl's resentment of his father any more unusual than that of a lonely, extremely sensitive, gifted child of quarreling, troubled parents?

Carl wrote that his "first communion had been a fatal experience for me. I was seized with the most vehement pity for my father. All at once I understood the tragedy of his profession and his life. He was struggling with a death whose existence he could not admit. An abyss had opened between him and me, and I saw no possibility of ever bridging it, for it was infinite in extent" (ibid., p. 73). It is reasonable to assume that in his life and his dreams Jung addressed the psychological bridge to his father more than he tells us. His father was both real and symbolic: John, Paul, Achilles, and Jung. Achilles, one of the great Greek heroes of the Battle of Troy, was slain by an arrow shot by Paris into his vulnerable heel. "My memory of my father is of a sufferer stricken with an Amfortas wound, a 'fisher king' whose wound would not heal, that Christian suffering for which the alchemists sought the panacea" (ibid., p. 242). In mythology, the Amfortas wound is received by the knight in quest of fame and caused by a poison spear thrown by a heathen adversary. Seen in this light, Jung was not powerless, like Parsifal, except in retrospect as a child: "I as a 'dumb' Parsifal was the witness of this sickness during the years of my boyhood and like Parsifal, speech failed me" (ibid.). In his maturity, Jung, like Parsifal, dared ask the question and thus began the healing of the fisher king within. Emma Jung and Marie-Louise von Franz explain that the "Grail is concerned with that stage of psychic development which, *after his earthly death* carries Christ's effectiveness *in this world*, and preserves his 'soul substance' throughout the ages" (Jung 1970, p. 156).

His father's woundedness may have been Carl's salvation: "Just as the wounded wounds himself, so the healer heals himself" (Jung 1969, p. 242).

There are alternative hypotheses (Chamberlin 1965) to the construct of the son's watching the father's death with a "clinical detachment and an obvious defense against what was certainly a chilling denouement to his father's ill-fated existence": Carl could have watched with awe, dread, denial, anger, helplessness, etc., in the face of death. His mother reminded him that his father had "died in time for you." Carl's rejuvenation after his father's death was not so remarkable as it was understandable and natural. Jung wrote that *Answer to Job* was foreshadowed by a significant dream; the compensation aspect seems self-evident:

> It started with my paying a visit to my long-deceased father. He was living in the country—I did not know where. I saw a house in the style of the eighteenth century, very roomy, with several rather large buildings. It had originally been, I learned, an inn at a spa, and it seemed that great personages, famous people and princes, had stopped there. Furthermore, several had died and their sarcophagi were in a crypt belonging to the house. My father guarded these as a custodian. He was, as I soon discovered, not only the custodian but also a distinguished scholar in his own right—which he had never been in his lifetime. (Jung 1969, pp. 244–267)

The long dream continues and Paul reveals great knowledge of the Old Testament. Jung was joined by a psychiatrist his age, and his son, also a psychiatrist. His father's

> argument was so intelligent and so learned that we in our stupidity could not follow it . . . his mind was flooded with profound ideas. I was annoyed and thought it was a pity that he had to talk in the presence of three such idiots as we . . . The dream discloses a thought and a premonition that have long been present in humanity: the idea of the creature that surpasses its creator by a small but decisive factor. (Ibid.)

Henri Ellenberger once met an old lady who had been well acquainted with Reverend Paul Jung in her youth. She described him as a "quiet, unassuming, kindhearted man who admirably knew how to preach to peasants and was universally loved and respected by his parishoners. (But) Paul Jung's colleagues considered him a somewhat boring man" (Ellenberger 1970, p. 662). Carl Jung summed it up this way: "I had a good personal relationship with my father, but no 'father complex' of the ordinary type. True, I didn't like theology because it set my father problems which *he* couldn't solve, and which *I* felt unjustified. On the other hand I grant you my mother complex" (Jung 1975, p. 65).

Stein's paper presents the concept that one can look at Jung's work as the therapy of Christianity, and that Jung's relationship with his father played the part of the central force in this destiny.

When his father was dying and asked Carl if he had passed his state examinations, "Carl duly lied. 'Yes. It went very well' " (Brome 1978, p. 61). That may not have been a lie—it may have been his truth about a different state, a different examination.

I recall that when my own father was dying of cancer I visited him at the Touro Infirmary in New Orleans. It was in 1940, just before Pearl Harbor, and I had flown from the Panama Canal Zone wearing my naval medical officer's uniform. I was on my way to a hospital where I would be confined to bed for eleven months. My father asked me how I was doing. "Very well," I said, "I have orders to sea." Thinking back on that time, I don't feel that I lied. In fact, the orders to sea came fifteen years later.[2]

> *It fortifies my soul to know*
> *that though I wander, truth is so.*
> A. H. Clough

References

Brome, Vincent. 1978. *Jung*. New York: Atheneum.
Chamberlin, T. C. 1965. The method of multiple working hypotheses. *Science* 148:754–759.
Ellenberger, Henri. 1970. *The Discovery of the Unconscious*. New York: Basic Books, Inc.
Jung, C. G. 1949. Foreword to *The Significance of the Father in the Destiny of the Individual. Collected Works* 4:301–323. Princeton, N.J.: Princeton University Press, 1961.
———. 1969. *Memories, Dreams, Reflections*. London: Collins/Fontana Library.
———. 1975. *Letters*. Vol. 2, 1951–1961. Princeton, N.J.: Princeton University Press.
Jung, Emma and Marie-Louise von Franz. 1970. *The Grail Legend*. New York: Putnam's Sons.
Oeri, Albert. 1970. Some youthful memories of C. G. Jung. *Spring*, 182–189.
Santayana, George. 1930. *The Realm of Truth*. Book Three of *Realms of Being*. New York: Scribner's.

---

[2]   I was back in the Navy during the Korean War Emergency, and while stationed at the Naval Medical Research Institute, Bethesda, MD, received orders to the U.S.S. Forrestal on its shake-down cruise from Norfolk, VA. It would be more appropriate to say that I understood my comment to my father forty-four years later, twenty-eight years after the orders came, because I fully understood it only as I wrote this paper—when I saw that I had written "I received my orders to *see*."